what's your excuse
for not
clearing your clutter

what's your excuse ...

FOR
NOT

CLEARING YOUR
CLUTTER?

Overcome your excuses, simplify your life,
make space for what matters

juliet landau-pope

"This may be the only organising book you will ever need! Juliet has the experience and insight to help readers understand their relationship with clutter, and practical tips to put to immediate use for instant results"

Laurene Livesey Park, certification program director,
ICD Institute for Challenging Disorganization

"Wow, what an excellent book! Spot on with all the examples, suggestions and situations. These excuses will certainly resonate with anyone who wants to declutter and will help them to stay motivated"

Ingrid Jansen, director, Organise Your House; president,
APDO Association of Professional Declutterers & Organisers

"This compact and powerful book is infused with compassion, supported by research and reflects industry best practices. It's a gem. If you feel trapped in clutter, do yourself the greatest service: read this book!"

Alison Lush CPO-CD, professional organiser specialising in
chronic disorganisation

"Once again Juliet provides a perfect blend of compassion and knowledge to make scary tasks doable. Her tone whispers encouragement and her intelligent spin on decluttering make it all very manageable. A must-read!"

Rivka Caroline, productivity consultant; director,
SoBe Organized

"As in her one-to-one sessions, Juliet challenges the received wisdom of the personal organising industry. She doesn't insist you throw out anything; rather she has the wit and sensitivity to recognise what you are trying to make space for in your life and offers practical solutions to get you there"

Jenni Muir, writer and restaurant consultant

"A book to read in one go and then refer to over and over again. Clear answers to questions without making you feel silly. A must for anyone who lives in the twenty-first century. A tonic for the soul!"

Ronit Knoble, producer and director, Fantastic Films

"Juliet has a logical, no-nonsense approach to decluttering which will help readers to declutter properly, without feeling overwhelmed or frustrated. A brilliant, helpful guide!"

Shelina Jokhiya, professional organiser and director, DeCluttr Me

Also by this author

Being More Productive   Time Mgt

Also in this series

Living a Life You Love
— Getting Fit
Overcoming Stress
Being Better With Money
Loving Your Job
— Eating Healthily
Being More Confident
Getting Your Dream Job

What's Your Excuse for not Clearing Your Clutter?

This first edition published in 2018 by WYE Publishing
9 Evelyn Gardens, Richmond TW9 2PL
www.wyepublishing.com

ISBN 978-0-9956052-4-4

Cover and text design by Annette Peppis & Associates

'What's Your Excuse…?' is a UK Registered Trade Mark
(Registration No: 3018995)

www.whatsyourexcuse.co.uk
Follow What's Your Excuse…? on Twitter – @whats_yr_excuse
www.facebook.com/whatsyourexcusebooks

www.jlpcoach.com
Follow Juliet on Twitter – @jlpcoach

Printed and bound in Great Britain by
Marston Book Services Ltd, Oxfordshire

Contents

Introduction

How this book will help you

Are your wardrobes crammed full of clothes, yet you can't find anything to wear?

Do you waste time, money or energy looking for documents buried in piles of other papers?

Or maybe you're storing a surfeit of things behind closed doors, boxed under beds, lurking in the loft or stuffed into a cupboard where they are out of sight but not out of mind?

Holding onto personal belongings which are no longer used or needed can become a habit and over time it can have a significant impact. If you're eager to clear your clutter but feel stuck or don't know where to start, I can help.

For almost a decade I've helped hundreds of people from diverse backgrounds to simplify their lives by decluttering space and schedules. From parents of young children whose homes have been taken over by toys to elderly people facing downsizing decisions to professionals trying to work from home in messy offices, one thing is clear: clutter represents an overload of logistical and emotional challenges. And if you're dealing with a painful transition such as bereavement, separation or divorce, the difficulties of controlling clutter can be particularly acute.

The first thing to emphasize about clutter is that it's not about your stuff – it's all about you. My aim is to help you to review your behaviour and beliefs rather than your belongings.

I leave it to you to define what you regard as clutter. I honestly don't have an opinion on how much of anything you 'should' keep. If you're happy with your wall-to-wall collection of books or bags my role is not to persuade you to part from them.

I won't promise to transform your living space into something which resembles a feature in a glossy magazine. Anyone who's set foot in my own home will confirm that I don't belong to the tidy brigade.

Instead, I'd like to invite you to join a conversation, one which raises questions about ingrained habits. Rather than prescribe a one-size-fits-all method, I'll ask you to reflect on questions to help you to review your perspective and to find bespoke solutions which suit you and your household. The emphasis is not on magical makeovers but on lasting and sustainable change. There are no quick fixes but recognising your excuses and reframing your answers is a vital step in the right direction.

If you're ready to rethink and reform your relationship with stuff, read on.

What is clutter?

We live in a society where shopping has become a leisure activity. We no longer only purchase things we need and thanks to incessant advertising we're constantly under pressure to acquire more and more. Whether it's kitting ourselves out with fashionable 'must-have' items or upgrading technology that's outdated before we open the box, our homes become over-filled by a steady stream of new stuff. As globalisation drives down prices, ever-more sophisticated marketing convinces us to buy more than ever.

Add to this the things which other people bring into our lives, albeit with the best of intentions, such as gifts, inheritances, souvenirs and things left for safekeeping and we're battling on all fronts against a constant onslaught of clutter – excess stuff which we don't need or want. No wonder so many of us feel that we are losing control.

Journalist and author James Wallman invented the word 'stuffocation' to describe the crisis generated by this rampant materialism. Put simply, buying stuff is not making us happier; it's heightening stress, harming relationships and causing untold damage to the environment.[1]

---

1   James Wallman, *Stuffocation: Living More With Less*, Penguin, 2015

A radically alternative trend has recently emerged, led by activists and bloggers who call themselves minimalists. As Fumio Sasaki explains in his book, Goodbye Things, minimalists reject pressure to conspicuously and compulsively consume:

'Our worth is not the sum of our belongings. Possessions can make us happy only for brief periods. Unnecessary material objects suck up our time, our energy and our freedom'[2]

This is a powerful message but who's to say what is necessary or excessive? Necessary for what? Our relationship to things is complex because they serve so many different functions.

Throughout my career as a university lecturer, life coach and professional organiser I've explored the meanings we attribute to material things. I'm also fascinated by the role of motivation: what drives us forward and what inspires us to change.[3] There's no doubt that the way we manage time and space is intrinsically linked. The physical environment in which we live, work, sleep, play and relax impacts mood

2   Fumio Sasaki, Goodbye, Things: On Minimalist Living, Random House, 2017
3   Read more about this in my first book, What's Your Excuse for not Being More Productive? WYE Publishing, 2017

and mindset, which in turn affects productivity and wellbeing.

Through conversations with clients and colleagues I've learned that clutter is never just stuff – it represents a tangled mass of anxieties, aspirations, fears and fantasies. It links us through memory to the past and through hope to the future. And it helps us to maintain emotional connections to distant places associated with family, faith, culture and identity. The things which we collect and keep all have meanings, both personal and social.

> The things which we collect and keep all have meanings

Clutter, I believe, is a very subjective concept. Only *you* can determine whether you have too many cookbooks, coloured pencils, pet toys or pyjamas. The key question is whether the amount of stuff in your home interferes with what you want to do or who you want to be. That's why I choose to define clutter as whatever is getting in your way, in your home or in your head.

What impact does clutter have?

At the beginning of the novel Anna Karenina, Leo Tolstoy observed that 'All happy families are alike; each unhappy family is unhappy in its own way'. If Tolstoy had been a professional organiser, he might have observed that all orderly spaces were similar but each cluttered space was cluttered in its own way.

Tolerance levels for clutter differ enormously. Your partner might be oblivious to bicycles, prams and scooters in the hallway while you bristle with irritation as soon as you step through the front door. One flat-sharer might be able to ignore piles of unopened post while another can't rest if there's one stray envelope on a table. These differences occur in the workplace too. I've visited offices where some staff members embrace a 'clear desk' policy while others function best when surrounded by books, papers and files.

Sensitivities can vary according to location too. Are you relaxed about the tower of books on your bedside table but frustrated by the build-up of foodstuffs on kitchen worktops? Can you cope with clothes thrown on a stool in your bedroom but not with walking boots abandoned in the lounge?

Responses to clutter aren't always rational or consistent but the impact can be profound. Here are some of the most common effects. Do any of these resonate with you?

- **Inconvenience**

  This is particularly relevant in smaller homes or narrow spaces where clutter restricts access but even in more spacious properties it limits functionality. No matter the size of your kitchen, for example, if it feels cluttered you won't enjoy cooking or entertaining. Likewise, if your guest room has turned into a dumping ground, you'll be less ready for visitors

- **Mood**

  Just as colour, design and layout of space influence your feelings, so too does material stuff. People who sense that there's too much stuff in their bedroom report that it impacts on quality of sleep.[4] And waking up in a room which feels cluttered is not conducive to a restful or productive day

---

4   Pamela Thaker, *Sleep Quality and Sleep Disturbance in Those at Risk of Hoarding Disorder for SLEEP 2015 (conference of sleep experts), Washington DC*

● Health and safety

If you've ever fallen over toys in the lounge or stepped on a piece of Lego, you'll appreciate the physical risks. Clutter creates hazards especially for vulnerable people such as children, the elderly and anyone with restricted mobility. These include fire and trip hazards, and increased likelihood of vermin and infestations. A messy home is harder to clean, leading to dust, grime and dirt which can also impact health

● Finances

Do you waste money replacing clothes or accessories which you already own because you can't locate them or forget that you've already bought them? If you can't see what's in kitchen cabinets, you'll also waste money on goods which you already stock. You may pay a heavy price for missing payment deadlines if you lose important paperwork. Clutter could also get in the way of generating income from your home by renting out a spare room, for example

● Waste

If your fridge is too full it's hard to keep track of what you're consuming and what you have left. Chances are you'll end up with goods past their sell-by date which may then get thrown away. The same is true for frozen food and if your appliances are over-stocked they won't function optimally

- **Relationships**
  Clutter can be a major source of tension between partners, family members, lodgers or sharers. Even if you live alone, if you're self-conscious about the amount of stuff in your home it can inhibit your social life. That's why professional organisers refer to CHAOS: Can't Have Anyone Over Syndrome

- **Time**
  Clutter is intrinsically linked to problems of time management – it can be both a source and a symptom of procrastination. You might be avoiding or delaying a vital task because you can't face looking for something which is lost in clutter or because you feel overwhelmed

- **Emotions**
  Feelings of guilt or shame often accrue with clutter: embarrassment is a common theme. Clutter can also become part of a demoralising cycle of thoughts and behaviour, perpetuating feelings of inadequacy which can have far-reaching consequences

Tackling your clutter will help you to regain control of your home and boost your motivation to create positive changes in other areas of your life. Don't take my word for it. Try it and see!

What is decluttering?

Professional organisers worldwide are immensely grateful to Marie Kondo, the media sensation from Japan who has done more to promote the organising industry in the last few years than any other individual.[5] While I admire her energy, commitment and business acumen, I don't share her approach. The method – so popular that her name is used in some circles as a verb – comprises a regimental system of sorting possessions according to a strict ordering system and judging their worth according to whether or not they 'spark joy'.

This clearly works for her fans but it's not for everyone. For some, Kondo's recommendations are difficult to follow without practical or emotional support. I've also witnessed adverse reactions to her perfectionist tendencies; people who can't attain or maintain her standards can end up feeling even more stressed, anxious or inadequate.

By contrast, my approach starts with a conversation rather than a set of directives. How do you feel about your home? How do you visualise the changes you

---

5   *http://tidyingup.com*

want to create? And what prompts you to think about decluttering now?

There's more to decluttering in my view than tidying up. My aim is to empower you to develop routines to manage time and space more effectively, and to free yourself of limiting stories. It's a journey of self-reflection which builds confidence and clarity. In other words, it's about shifting both physical and emotional clutter.

The latest wave of decluttering manuals from Sweden has adopted the slogan 'death cleaning'.[6] They promote a brand of minimalism: simplifying stuff as if in preparation for the end of life. I've been engaged in this kind of work for years already, helping elderly people to downsize their homes or to make room (literally) for live-in care. Awareness of mortality, at any age, is a powerful motivator. I prefer however to call this life clearing because it produces clarity during the lifetime of a person, not during their demise.

The process of decluttering will vary for every individual but it is likely to include the following:

- Framing positive goals and visualising success: defining your purpose
- Taking stock: reviewing what you own
- Sorting things into categories

6   *Margareta Magnusson, The Gentle Art of Swedish Death Cleaning, Canongate, 2017*

- Making active choices about what to keep and what to reuse, recycle, donate or discard
- Finding meaningful ways to part with things you no longer want or need
- Celebrating achievements – it's progress which matters, not perfection

While decluttering you'll almost certainly part from things but I never talk about 'getting rid' of anything because it's disrespectful towards your belongings. And I've never ever hired a skip.

I take the view that everything comes into your life for a reason but there's no imperative to keep it forever.

I encourage you to approach decluttering with kindness and compassion. Let go of self-criticism and be kind to yourself. Accept that acquisitions were well-intentioned and that mistakes, such as buying shoes you don't wear or exercise machines you don't use, are human. Set aside self-judgement and focus on your positive goals.

> Let go of self-criticism and be kind to yourself

Decluttering is not a project but rather a lifestyle choice. Think about how long it took to accumulate your stuff. Chances are it didn't arrive in your home in one fell swoop so reducing it will be a gradual and ongoing process. Over time it will change the way you relate to material possessions and your physical environment, changing the way you shop, how you enjoy your home and what you share with others.

Finally, it's important to distinguish between decluttering and organising. The main purpose of this book is to motivate you to reduce surplus stuff. Only then does it make sense to think about storage solutions and systems to maintain order.

Whose clutter is it anyway?

As the title of this book suggests, my aim is first and foremost to help you to clear *your* clutter. Even if you're driven to distraction by things which belong to other members of your household, I advise you *not* to sort stuff without the full cooperation and involvement of their owners. There's no doubt that disputes over clutter can be a major source of tension between those who live or work together. But as a professional organiser and parent, I believe it's imperative to respect things which belong to others. Decluttering without their consent, whatever your motive, can undermine trust and damage relationships; it's also likely to backfire and will be futile if you're aiming for long-term change.

Use the advice in this book to tackle your own personal clutter and your example is likely to motivate others.

The good news

Think back to how you learned to shop. Perhaps you accompanied a parent on a trip to the high street or market? Or maybe you calculated the cost of goods while practising basic maths? You may even have played at being a shop-keeper in nursery school. You likely also witnessed the exchange of gifts at birthday parties and seasonal celebrations. From an early age we are taught how to behave as consumers and as we grow up these messages are reinforced through education and media as well as our own experiences.

Many cultures have customs to mark the acquisition of something new – when I was growing up, whenever a family member wore a new item of clothing they'd be greeted with an expression translated from Yiddish: 'Wish you well to wear it' or 'Wear it in good health'.

What we don't learn routinely, however, is how to let go of clutter. I haven't yet come across any children's games associated with sorting, selecting or streamlining material possessions. Nor have I heard of any rituals or blessings to celebrate parting from things.

The good news is that it's never too late to learn. My work often involves coaching parents to involve children in keeping their space clutter-free. I've taught teenagers to reclaim messy rooms and coached octogenarians to purge paperwork. At any age or stage of life, organising and decluttering skills *can* be improved. Like any new skill set they take time, patience and practice to hone; change doesn't happen overnight. But if you're ready to kick clutter to the kerb, you too can enjoy the benefits. These include:

- A greater sense of control over your space
- Light and clarity
- Calm and relaxation
- Pride in and enjoyment of your home
- Less stress and worry
- Harmony among household members
- Improved quality of sleep
- Motivation to cook and entertain
- More time and energy to spend on what really matters

Many clients say that decluttering is akin to losing weight – it makes them feel physically lighter and more energetic. Others talk about experiencing a sense of liberation and relief.

Whatever your personal goals, I invite you to frame them in positive terms. Don't dwell on what you're likely to lose but focus on what will become possible. What will you enjoy and appreciate about your clutter-free space? It's impossible to predict all the outcomes but trust that you're creating positive changes.

What are excuses?

Being asked, 'What's your excuse?' might feel a little uncomfortable. But my intention is not to judge or put you on the defensive. I'm simply inviting you to explore the stories which you tell yourself. Excuses, I believe, are just stories which we construct to explain or validate situations in which we find ourselves.

These stories become increasingly familiar over time. As we repeat them – to others or to ourselves – we become attached to them and, like clutter, they become hard to shift. They may serve a purpose at some point in our lives but become outdated or redundant as time goes on.

The excuses outlined in this book are all based on beliefs about things, people or relationships between them. Exploring the assumptions underpinning these beliefs opens up new perspectives. And as perspectives shift, so can habits.

Indeed, when we start to look critically at stories we tell about the world and our place in it, anything becomes possible. As Rosamund Stone Zander and Benjamin Zander say:

'Many of the circumstances that seem to block us in our daily lives may only appear to do so based on a framework of assumptions we carry with us. Draw a different frame around the same set of circumstances and new pathways come into view. Find the right framework and extraordinary accomplishment becomes an everyday experience'[7]

Even the most daunting of decluttering projects can feel more manageable with a change of perspective.

---

7   Rosamund Stone Zander and Benjamin Zander, The Art of Possibility: Transforming Professional and Personal Life, Penguin, 2002

How to use this book

The purpose of this book is twofold: to address procrastination around clutter and to set out practical strategies for dealing with it.

In the first three chapters of this book I outline the most common excuses for not dealing with clutter, invite you to consider some alternative viewpoints and share some tips to help you to think and act differently.

The next sections focus on various specific categories of clutter. The problems in these sections – and the proposed solutions – are fairly ubiquitous so if you don't find an answer to a particular clutter quandary in one chapter you might find it in another.

One excuse can also mask another, or link to others. I've tried to tease out different strands, presenting them separately in order to provide a more focused set of responses.

The "Next Steps" section includes suggestions on how to dispose of things which you no longer want or need and on how to prevent it piling back up again. Like weight management, it's important to think about maintenance so that you can enjoy long-term benefits.

Feel free to dip in and out of various sections and

to read in any order you choose. The index may help you to locate the information you most need to. Don't worry if you don't read through the book from start to finish. I didn't write it in a linear fashion and there's no obligation to read it that way!

My aim is to kick start you into action so if you're compelled while reading to put the book down and start clearing your clutter instead, please let me know. I'll be delighted.

And finally, if you've found this book useful, please don't leave it on your shelves to gather dust. Demonstrate your commitment to decluttering by passing it on to someone else!

The Excuses

Self-Beliefs

I'm a bit of a hoarder

When I'm introduced as a declutter coach people often jest that their partner, sibling or best friend could do with my help because they're a 'bit of a hoarder'. Often delivered with a nervous laugh, it's also a phrase I frequently hear from people who phone to inquire about the services I offer. But in most cases the label isn't accurate or helpful.

It's a sensitive topic which is often misunderstood. Hoarding syndrome was recently recognised by the National Health Service as a specific and complex mental health disorder.[8] Symptoms include a disproportionate attachment to material things, an excessive number of belongings and in some instances an addiction to shopping.

But having a messy playroom, an untidy bedroom or a disorganised home office doesn't make you a hoarder. Like many professional organisers I prefer to use the term 'clutterbug' for people who own more than they need or who feel overwhelmed by levels of disorder.

---

8   *https://www.nhs.uk/conditions/hoarding-disorder*

The key difference between a hoarder and a clutterbug in my experience is not the volume of possessions, but rather the ability to let things go.

The vast majority of people whose homes I help to declutter are everyday clutterbugs rather than hoarders, overwhelmed by too much stuff but ready to review and reduce. So if you're using this excuse, even in jest, I gently encourage you to rethink the label you've adopted.[9]

I'm too sentimental

Nostalgia is a powerful emotion but let it fill your heart, not your home.

If you're holding onto things that have sentimental value, ask yourself these questions:

- What really matters – the thing itself or the person who gave it to you, the place where you bought it or the event which it commemorates?
- What price are you paying in terms of space? Consider the broader implications of dwelling on the past

9   *For a more detailed discussion of hoarding disorder see Jo Cooke, Understanding Hoarding, Sheldon Press, 2017*

- What are you most afraid of losing – the item or the memory it triggers?
- Do you really need the object to recall these memories?

Your answers may steer you towards letting go of at least some of your sentimental clutter. Don't be too ambitious, just aim to reduce the amount slightly. Take photos of things which you feel ready to part from so that you and your family will have a record.

As for storing things of sentimental value from which you're not yet ready to part, have you thought of creating a memory box? But make active choices about how many keepsakes to store; remember that when everything is special, nothing is special.

I'm naturally disorganised

The US-based Institute for Challenging Disorganization outlines four features of chronic disorganisation:

- Long-term disorganisation over many years
- A detrimental impact on quality of life
- Frequent (and futile) efforts at self-help
- Low expectations of change

The good news is that even if these resonate with you, you can still learn techniques to manage time and space more effectively.

This story about one of my clients might inspire you:

Annie was a fifty year-old actress who enlisted my help to sort out her kitchen. Worktops were strewn with old magazines, household bills and out-of-date tins. As Annie showed me around she berated herself for being disorganised. 'I'm a lost cause', she joked. 'If you can memorise your lines for an entire Shakespeare play', I responded, 'you have the skills to remember where to put away things'. This clearly resonated. Together, we cleared clutter and devised simple routines to keep surfaces clear. It was only by letting go of the 'disorganised' label that Annie felt able to tackle these tasks.

Think about labels which you've attached to yourself and how they are now holding you back. Like clutter, these labels accumulate over time and become part of our 'emotional baggage'. There may be an element of truth but it's always worth looking for evidence to contradict the story you're telling yourself.

Strategy

I don't know where to start

As with any major project, it's important to plan first steps. I recommend starting somewhere where you can make a visible impact but which won't be too demanding emotionally. Here are some ideas:

* **Hallway**

  The entrance to your home makes a major impression on you and on your visitors. Do bulky items such as bicycles, prams or scooters really need to be parked there? Do all the hats, coats, scarves and gloves belong in the hall? Could items which are not in current use be stored elsewhere? What about sportswear which only goes out to play periodically?

* **Lounge or family room**

  A room where you spend lots of time can also be a good place to start. Question whether all of the furniture has a clear purpose. Do you love it and use it? Does it still suit your taste and lifestyle? I suggest clearing away anything – books, papers, toys –

which doesn't belong on the carpet. Measuring results in terms of visible floorspace can be very rewarding

- **Bedrooms**
  The room in which you sleep should be a restful environment. Waking up in a room which feels uncluttered is also likely to boost your mood and your motivation. Start by taking stock of the largest and most dominating items in the room: is there a chair which is serving as a clutter magnet for clothes which haven't yet found their way to the laundry, some long-neglected exercise equipment, or suitcases which haven't been put away since your last trip?

- **Kitchen**
  Often the hub of a home, the kitchen can be a clutter hotspot. If you enjoy cooking or eating in your kitchen, you'll have more incentive to tackle this room first. Start with surfaces, including worktops, tables and space above the fridge. Take a critical look at gadgets and gizmos that are rarely, if ever used. Clearing magnets and notes from the fridge can make a quick and visible difference

Here's how one of my clients got started:

Lisa contacted me because she was preparing to relocate abroad with her husband and young family. It was a stressful time: she was busy researching new schools, childcare and business opportunities so was feeling overwhelmed. Meanwhile, all the rooms in her home were full of regular household stuff which needed sorting. After some discussion, I suggested that we start by clearing her bedroom. She desperately needed a haven, a room in which she could relax and think through decisions. Decluttering her bedroom therefore helped her to prepare physically and emotionally for the move.

If you're dealing with changes in your life, you may also need space to think. Clutter can be a huge distraction so organising just one room, or even a corner, will help.

Don't ruminate too long over where to start, just pick somewhere where you'll see the results fairly quickly. What's important is to take those first vital steps.

I'll make even more of a mess

It's a harsh reality that things sometimes have to get worse before they get better. If you need to empty wardrobes or clear out cabinets, there is no way to avoid some temporary disorder so be prepared:

- Pace yourself and allow plenty of time to make decisions
- Have realistic expectations about what you can achieve in one session
- Have bags ready for rubbish, recycling and donations and clear them at the end of each session
- Celebrate every achievement, even if you've liberated just one bookshelf
- If the room looks chaotic, remember it's a work in progress

Whether you're looking forward to cooking in a clutter-free kitchen, waking up in a bedroom which feels clear and airy or simply feeling more in control of your physical environment, hold onto your vision of success. You might make some mess before achieving your goals but it will be worth it in the end.

There are too many decisions to make

What to keep and what to let go? How to dispose of things you don't want and how to organise those that you do? What happens if you make a mistake? Clutter, I believe, is a tangled mass of delayed decisions. And it's not surprising that it often builds up when you're distracted. You might also be over-thinking. Incessantly weighing up pros and cons can lead to 'analysis paralysis'.

It's hard to make decisions when there are many other demands on time, energy and attention. That's one of the reasons that people experiencing transitions such as separation, divorce, bereavement or downsizing feel daunted by clutter. The same is true after having a baby or returning to work after maternity leave.

> Clutter, I believe, is a tangled mass of delayed decisions

So how to embrace actions which involve choices and become a more confident decision maker? One way is to focus on just one specific category of clutter at a time and adopt a simple sorting system. Instead of reviewing your entire shoe collection, for example, look solely (no pun intended!) at sandals. Resolve in advance how you will make decisions. Establish clear and simple criteria such as: Do they fit? Are they comfortable? Will I have an occasion on which to wear them? Do I have a similar pair? It might be helpful to write down the questions you will ask yourself about each pair.

The following exercise will also dispel some anxiety around decisions:

Take note of all the micro-decisions you make throughout the day, from choosing what to wear, what to eat for breakfast, how to navigate your way to work. Notice the criteria you apply as you make up your mind. Train yourself to become more mindful about the choices you make; flex that decision-making muscle in order to strengthen it.

I don't want to contribute to landfill

If concern for the environment is hindering your efforts to declutter and if you're holding on to things you no longer need because you don't know how to dispose of them ethically, consider the impact this is having on your own personal environment.

I always aim to minimise rubbish while decluttering but it's not usually possible to avoid it altogether. If you're keen to reduce household clutter you can find ways to recycle and reuse but be pragmatic too – a zero-waste policy may not be realistic.

For more information on disposal strategies see "Next Steps" towards the end of this book.

P 127

I can't face the cupboard of doom

Is there an area in your home which has been cluttered for so long that you dread even opening the door? Has the space under your stairs become a cupboard of doom? While you might joke about it the way you think and talk about this space may be detrimental. It's a reminder of the negativity you associate with clutter. It's also undermining any motivation you may have to change it. Would calling it the 'storage space' or simply 'under the stairs' make it less intimidating?

By the same token, referring to your spare room as the 'junk room' is an unintentional way of validating the current state of clutter. If you want to shift the junk, it helps to clarify what purpose you'd like the room to fulfil. Start calling it the 'guest room' or the 'art room' or the 'study' and you'll find it easier to visualise the space you want to create.

HOMES ARE SHRINKING

New homes are 20 per cent smaller than they were in the Seventies, a study has found. Kitchens are 25 per cent smaller, while bedrooms and bathrooms have 20 per cent less space.

"Yours" magazine 8/01/18

Situation

I don't have enough storage

Newly-built houses in the UK are the smallest in Europe so it's not surprising there's little space in which to store anything.[10] However lack of storage is a complaint I hear from clients residing in all sorts of properties: old and new, sprawling mansions and studio flats.

If you struggle to find storage space I invite you to look critically at your possessions before buying storage products – you may simply have too much stuff. However if storage space really is an issue for you here are some suggestions to increase it in your home:

* **Under beds**
  Feng shui fans claim that under-bed storage interferes with energy flow and reduces sleep quality but for many people this is a useful space to store things which are only used occasionally. My preference is for large transparent boxes on wheels which can be pulled out easily

---

10   http://www.cam.ac.uk/research/news/study-finds-premise-behind-bedroom-tax-is-fundamentally-flawed

• **Shelving**

If you're buying ready-made units, check that shelves are easily adjustable so that you can adapt them to your needs

• **Wardrobes**

Opt for versatility. If there's one rail to hang clothes, is there space to add another lower or higher to double up? Maximise space by decluttering bulky hangers and putting boxes or baskets on the floor of the wardrobe

• **Cabinets and drawers**

Separate different categories of stuff, perhaps by using dividers, boxes or baskets. Even if Marie Kondo's tidying up regime doesn't appeal to you, her folding techniques work wonders.[11] For practical tips on how to fold essential items, such as fitted sheets, watch the videos made by my fellow organiser Ingrid Jansen[12]

• **Doors**

While you may not admire the aesthetic, it's better to hang things up than drape them over furniture

---

11   Marie Kondo, Spark Joy: An Illustrated Guide to the Japanese Art of Tidying, Vermilion, 2015
12   https://www.organiseyourhouse.co.uk/top-tips

or drop them on the floor. There's no need to attach hooks or rails – look for over-door products such as hanging shoe organisers

* **Boxes and baskets**
  Consider using shoe boxes, chocolate boxes or biscuit tins to provide innovative storage solutions for small items which would otherwise be scattered over surfaces

If once you've considered all of these suggestions you still don't feel you have enough space, check out my advice on using self-storage facilities in "Next Steps".

My partner has too much stuff

Are you exasperated by stuff which belongs to other members of your household? Are you and your partner at loggerheads over clutter which threatens your space and your sanity? In my experience, clutter is one of the most pervasive sources of tension between couples who live together.

Problems often occur when one partner is more sensitive to the build-up than the other. As noted earlier, it's not right or realistic to clear other people's belongings (see "Whose clutter is it anyway?" at the beginning of this book).

Here are some tips to help you cope:

* Take responsibility for dealing with your own clutter. Take a long, hard look at your own clothes, shoes, paperwork, etc. Set your own house (or part of it) in order
* Lead by example. Enthuse about the process and demonstrate the benefits of simplifying your space and your schedule
* Praise their progress – if your partner takes any steps to declutter, however small, encourage them to continue by acknowledging their effort

And here are a few suggestions of what *not* to do:

* Don't lecture others about decluttering. It will only bore or annoy them
* Don't ask rhetorical questions such as 'Why can't you sort this out?' These are impossible to answer and likely to create frustration and resentment on both sides
* Don't pressure your partner to part from anything. When you treat their belongings with respect they're more likely to listen and cooperate

Here's how two of my clients dealt with this situation:

Tanya was irritated by the mountain bikes, pumps and helmets which her partner Tom routinely parked in their hallway. They were not only unsightly, they also obstructed the entrance to their home. Underlying Tanya's irritation was resentment at Tom's cycling hobby because the bikes were expensive and took Tom away from home at weekends. For Tom, each bike was a thing of beauty and he didn't understand Tanya's intolerance. I sat down with the couple and invited them to listen to each other without judgement. We decluttered the dispute itself by separating the disparate strands: how much time to spend together as a family, how much money to spend on individual hobbies, and how to manage their shared space. Tom was persuaded to store some of his clobber in the garden shed while Tanya acknowledged how cycling helped him to keep fit and to cope with his stressful job.

As I often say, clutter is never just stuff but the meanings we attribute to our belongings are not always apparent to others. If you and partner are at loggerheads over clutter, make time to talk frankly but constructively. Focus on being smart rather than right. This means finding practical solutions rather than scoring points, and aiming for compromise rather than victory for either one of you.

I don't have time

Lack of time is one of the most common excuses for putting things off. As a result time management has become an industry: books, blogs, podcasts and planning tools all sell the idea that time can somehow be manipulated or mastered. Unfortunately the reality is that we can't manage time, we can only change the way we use it.

> We can't manage time, we can only change the way we use it

When time is at a premium, the only things you'll get done are the ones which you prioritise. Planning is also key. So instead of bemoaning a lack of time identify the decluttering tasks which matter most and allocate specific blocks of time to tackle them.

It may be difficult to predict precisely how long it will take to clear clutter in specific areas of your home – it will depend on your pace, stamina and ability to make decisions – but allocate some time to at least make a start. There's no need to wait for a large block of time entirely free of other commitments to materialise. Carve out small chunks of time and set yourself micro-goals such as clearing the contents of one drawer or sorting things into piles. Challenge yourself by setting a timer. You'll be amazed at what you can achieve in just fifteen minutes.

For more tips on making the most of your time see my first book, What's Your Excuse for not Being More Productive?[13]

---

13   *What's Your Excuse for not Being More Productive? WYE Publishing, 2017*

Clothes

How often do you stare at your over-stuffed wardrobe and complain that you can't find anything to wear? Or maybe your clothes are languishing on chairs and chests in your room, or piling up in a 'floordrobe'?

Clothes, I believe, are imbued with complex meanings: they not only represent your own individual style and personality but also signify links to social groups and communities. From headscarves to football shirts or sarees to sportswear, clothes reflect how we see ourselves and how we want to be seen by others. As with other forms of clutter, they also connect us to memories of the past and visions of the future. No wonder we find it so difficult to let them go.

I'm hoping to lose weight

It's well known that most people only wear between a quarter and a half of their clothes regularly. In my decluttering work I find that the reason for this is that many people (particularly women) have lots of clothes which simply don't fit. According to one study 85% of women own clothes which don't fit and three quarters of British women confess to owning a bra which they haven't worn for a year.[14]

As with other categories of clutter, there are no standard guidelines on how many clothes you 'should' keep. But the following questions will help you to reflect on your specific situation:

- The best method is to take everything out of the wardrobe. Put clothes which fit on one side of the room and those which don't on the other. What proportion are unwearable? If this exercise is too daunting tackle one category at a time, for instance shirts, dresses or trousers

- Do you have a name for the clothes which don't fit? Do you distinguish between 'fat clothes' and 'skinny clothes'? Here's the paradox: while clients often claim that they're keeping skinny jeans to motivate them to diet, the reality is that they don't provide any incentive at all. How long have some of those clothes hung in your wardrobe? If they haven't motivated you up to now, how likely are they to do so in the future? Consider the price you're paying in terms of negative energy and self-criticism

---

14   *Elizabeth Bye and Ellen McKinney, Sizing up the Wardrobe: Why We Keep Clothes That Do Not Fit,* Fashion Theory*, Vol. 11, Issue 4, 2007*

Here's how one of my clients overcame this issue:

Sharona hired me to help her declutter after her divorce. Her wardrobe was full of clothes which were at least two sizes too small; she'd gained weight due to stress and was struggling to lose it. 'When I look at the jeans I can no longer wear, I want to cry', she said. Together we sorted her jeans according to size and counted the ones which were too tight. With a little encouragement, she picked out her favourite pair and put them up on a high shelf. As for the rest, she agreed to donate them to a local drop-in centre for refugees. Later that day Sharona phoned me to say, 'It was difficult to let go of my old clothes but now I feel liberated. It's as if a huge weight has been lifted from my shoulders'.

If you're holding onto clothes which don't fit, notice the impact they have on your mood. Decluttering will not only free up space in your wardrobe, it will also relieve you of negativity and shame. If you sell the clothes (online perhaps) you'll also have some money to spend on new items when you do lose weight. Keep a few choice items if you will but store these somewhere less prominent so that they won't confront you on a daily basis.

I'm hoping to gain weight

If you've experienced drastic weight loss you may be reluctant to part from clothes which are too roomy. You might associate them with a time when you felt or looked healthier or maybe there's a genuine expectation that you will return to a larger size. For elderly clients who find their frame shrinking, this can be a particularly poignant excuse for not decluttering.

My advice is to:

- Take stock of how many clothes you own which don't fit right now
- How likely are you to regain enough weight to look and feel good in these clothes?
- Are the colours and styles still likely to suit you?
- Could you possibly alter them or wear them with accessories such as belts, braces or scarves?
- Be selective and make positive choices. Consider keeping just a few of the items you most cherish

It's demoralising to see stacks of over-sized clothes in your wardrobe. Unless you're confident that you really will wear them again in the future, let them go.

It might come back into fashion one day

Fashions come and go but it might take years before you'll want to wear those mini-skirts or flared trousers. Is it worth living with clutter for years on the off-chance that you might wish to wear them again? Sparkly boob-tubes or jackets with enormous shoulder pads don't take up much space individually but wouldn't you rather have space for clothes you enjoy wearing *now*?

Give your retro clothing a new lease of life by offering them to a charity shop. Or if there's a theatre school or amateur dramatic group in your neighbourhood, you might be able to donate to their costume department.

If you can't bear to part from all your vintage gear, pick out just one or two items to keep. This will create more space in your current wardrobe and enable you to see and find the things which belong in your present rather than in your past.

I'm saving it for dressing up

If you have young children, you may be keeping certain clothes for them to dress up in. But there's no need to keep boxes or bags full of old sheets or over-sized shirts.

Here are some tips to help you cull the costumes:

- Designate a drawer or a box for dressing up clothes
- Only keep clean, good quality clothes. Discard anything smelly or musty
- Review stock at least once a year and declutter items which no longer fit your children

As for adults, fancy dress hire is easily available nowadays so if you don't have your personal stock of dressing up clothes you can always hire a costume.

It belonged to my grandmother

When my grandmother died at the age of ninety-four, I inherited a few treasured items: a cashmere beaded cardigan and a reversible jacket from Japan. I kept them for three decades but eventually decided to donate them to charity. Everything comes into our life for a reason but that doesn't mean we need to keep it all indefinitely. In my case, I realised that I didn't need these objects to remember my grandmother and since I couldn't wear them myself, I preferred to give them away and let someone else enjoy them.

Here are some tips:

- If you've inherited clothes, divide them into categories (dresses, suits, hats, etc) so that you can see how many of each you own. They may all have mattered to someone special in your life, but that doesn't mean you need to keep them all
- Are you likely to wear any yourself? If they don't fit or suit you in their current form, could they be altered so that you could wear them?
- Could they be offered to other family members (who might even wear them)?
- Select a few items, as I did, and keep them in safe storage, perhaps in a memory box
- If you're reluctant to part with an entire collection, adopt a more piecemeal approach. Find meaningful ways to let go of just a few things at a time (see "Disposal Strategies")

Ultimately, it's important to distinguish between the object and the person it belonged to. Donating your grandmother's clothes to charity is not an act of disloyalty. Before you part with them you might like to take photos to keep memories alive.

My mother made it

From hand-knitted sweaters which have lost their shape to clothes which you've never worn, garments made by people who you care about can be exceptionally difficult to let go.

My mother is a fashion designer and throughout my childhood she designed and made me beautiful clothes. For years I kept cocktail dresses which she'd made me for college balls and a tailored suit which I wore to my first job interview (yes, I got the job!) When I could no longer fit into the dresses and stopped going to such formal events I was faced with tough decisions. I chose to keep just the suit jacket. The others were donated to a charity shop.

Do you have clothes which were crafted with love? If so, here are my tips:

- Pick out those you still love and wear. Take a critical look at the others and consider giving them away to other relatives or to charity
- Cherish the relationship with the person who made it, not the item
- Do they need to know you're giving away their gift? If you don't volunteer the information, would they ever find out?

However sentimental you feel about a homemade gift, you're not obliged to keep it forever.

I wore it on my wedding day

For many brides, their wedding dress becomes the most expensive and cherished item in their wardrobe, or in the box under their bed. While wedding dresses hold special memories, there's no escaping the fact that they also take up a considerable amount of space.

If you're hoping that your daughter might wear it on her wedding day, you're making several assumptions. Have you asked her if she wants to wear your dress? If she does express an interest in it and has a home of her own perhaps she can take the dress off your hands and store it herself. If, on the other hand, she's still in primary school, consider whether you want to hold onto it for so many more years.

If you're unsure about what to do with your wedding dress, remember that you married your partner, not the outfit. Your wedding photos show how you were dressed so why not donate it to one of these special charities:

- Gift of a Wedding and Wish for a Wedding both arrange weddings at short notice for terminally ill

patients in hospitals or hospices[15]
* Heavenly Gowns make burial clothes for stillborn babies[16]
* Some charity shops such as Oxfam have bridal departments which sell donated wedding dresses as well as bridesmaids' outfits and accessories[17]

One of my clients sold her bridal dress to the costume department of a historical re-enactment society. To find local re-enactment groups visit the National Association of Re-enactment Societies website.[18]

Finally, if you want a souvenir of your wedding day, keep just a token from your outfit such as the veil and store it carefully in a memory box.

It's tatty but I might need it

Are you keeping tatty or worn items 'just in case' you need them in the future? Here's a list of items I would urge you to discard immediately:

---

15 *http://giftofawedding.org and http://www.wishforawedding.co.uk*
16 *http://heavenlygowns.co.uk*
17 *https://www.oxfam.org.uk/shop/bridal/wedding-dress-faqs*
18 *http://www.nares.org.uk*

- Laddered tights or stockings
- Single socks
- Uncomfortable or unattractive underwear
- Old shirts or trousers for gardening or decorating
- Belts and scarves you don't wear

Keeping 'spare' clothing often stems from a scarcity mindset, a worry that you might not have enough in the future. If you can become more accustomed to recognising abundance, you'll find it easier to let go of clutter.

I bought it on holiday

Beaded T-shirts, floaty kaftans, baseball caps with snappy slogans – we've all fallen prey to holiday shopping sprees. When you strolled through the picturesque street market it was hard to resist a bargain. And in truth, you did wear it once or twice while you were away. But since returning to cooler climes, there's been no opportunity to sport your colourful beachwear or Hawaiian-print shorts.

Hold onto memories, not clutter

My adage is: hold onto memories, not clutter. If you want to recall holidays or special moments, take photos. Then donate souvenirs to charity. And in future desist from buying clothes on holiday in the first place – they're destined to become clutter as soon as you unpack.

It just needs to be mended/ altered/cleaned

Are you clinging on to clothes with broken zips, torn hems or neglected stains? These items serve no purpose until they are repaired, so follow these tips:

* Out of sight is out of mind so take them out of your wardrobe immediately
* If you're capable of carrying out repairs yourself, schedule time to do so, or at least to make a start. If not, ask friends or neighbours to recommend a local service
* Take all items together to a dry cleaner, repairs service or tailor – it's a better use of your time, and perhaps you can negotiate a discount for multiple repairs
* If anything is beyond repair or the costs are prohibitive, find a textile recycling facility so that at least someone else can make use of the fabric

There's no point agonising over how something fell into disrepair or feeling guilty that you haven't fixed it until now. Let go of regrets and focus instead on what needs to be done and who can do it.

It was very expensive

Once you've paid for something and brought it home it no longer matters how costly it was. The harsh reality is that unless you can return it immediately to the shop you're not likely to get that money back. If you invested in it for a special occasion be glad that it served its purpose. No matter how much you cherish it you don't need to keep it forever.

As for any brand-new clothes in your wardrobe, the price you paid is also irrelevant. The designer coat you couldn't resist in the sales, or the impulse buy with the label attached – unless you know for certain you'll wear them on a specific occasion, why live with the constant reminder of an expensive mistake? Let go of any embarrassment, liberate your wardrobe of the clutter and learn from the experience.

No matter how much you cherish it you don't need to keep it forever

It's too good to give away

Charity shops desperately need quality stock – your donation will help to raise money for a worthy cause. Charity shops also enable students and others on low incomes to buy clothes, shoes or accessories at knockdown prices. It's a triple win situation. Even clothes they can't sell directly can often be sold for reuse or recycling. One of the most rewarding aspects of my work as a declutter coach is finding local charities who need specific types of clothing or household goods: homeless shelters, organisations who support refugees or victims of domestic violence, patients in hospitals or hospices, care homes, etc. Knowing that the winter coat you no longer wear will make a difference to another person can motivate you to give away things even if they were expensive.

So please don't hesitate to declutter because you believe only cheap items should be donated. Nothing, but nothing, is ever too good to give away to others.

Books

Many of the people who seek out my advice on decluttering have a special affinity with books, as do I. Despite technological advances and the availability of ever cheaper e-book readers, printed books aren't going out of fashion.

But while booksellers, publishers and authors rejoice, books are also one of the most problematic categories of clutter. My advice: support the publishing industry by buying new books but there's no need to retain them all indefinitely.

As with other categories of clutter, I don't have an opinion on precisely how many books anyone should own. But if they're double-parked or even triple-parked on bookshelves or stuffed into crates in the garage, basement or attic I question the point of keeping so many. If you really love books I encourage you to declutter surplus stock so that you can make space for new ones.

I ought to read them

Are your shelves heaving with worthy novels which make
you feel anxious because you haven't yet read them?
Maybe you purchased a best-seller recommended by
friends but haven't yet found the time or inclination
to look at it? Or perhaps you received gifts from well-
meaning relatives who misjudged your taste? How
these books found their way into your home is of little
relevance now. What matters is what purpose they
serve in your life right now. Unless you genuinely love
the books in your home or look forward to reading
them in the future, you're free to make choices. Let go
of anything which makes you feel inadequate or which
reminds you of pressure to conform.

I'll read them soon

Do you have growing piles of books which you intend to
read some time in the future? You might be planning to
catch up with the Booker prize shortlist during a summer
holiday or maybe you're dreaming of retirement, even
if it's decades away. No matter. Your book collection is
bound to include some which you know with certainty
you will read but also others which are destined

to remain unopened. Meanwhile, those unread books are taking up space and gathering dust. They may also be physically getting in the way, especially if they're stacked up on the floor.

If you have a penchant for purchasing books which never get read, you're not alone. In Japanese there's even a word: 'tsundoku', meaning a pile of unread books.[19]

Here are some suggestions to manage book clutter:

- Assign a 'to-read' shelf for books that you haven't yet read so you can locate them easily next time you're packing for a long train journey or holiday
- Before you visit a bookshop or start browsing online, check your to-read shelf. You might find it useful to keep a photo of it on your phone. This might deter you from buying more books, especially titles that you already own

I also recommend a periodic cull of your to-read shelf, perhaps before your birthday or other meaningful date. If you haven't read them within a year, give them to others or donate them to charity.

---

19   *The word is a hybrid of 'tsunde oku' (to let something pile up) and 'doku' (to read)*

I might re-read them

When you've completed a satisfying novel, it's tempting to imagine reading it again but be honest, how much time do you have to read and how likely are you to return to it? How many new books await your attention on your to-read shelf (see "I'll Read Them Soon"), as well as magazines, newsletters and online articles and blogs? It's also worth considering the physical condition of each book – if it's battered or tattered, if pages are yellowing or print is faded, would you want to read this particular copy again?

Be selective, pick out just a few old favourites and declutter the rest.

They might go out of print

You've toyed with the idea of giving away obscure novels by lesser-known authors which you haven't looked at in ages, but worry that you might not be able to replace them. What if you decided that you absolutely needed to read a book again but found that it was out of print?

Ask yourself:

•   Is it vital for you to own this particular book? What

meaning does it hold?

- If you haven't needed it for a while, what are the chances that you will need it in the future?
- What difference would it really make if you were unable to replace it in the future?

No one can predict the future but consider what price you're paying right now for keeping so many books? Are they taking up valuable space or contributing to arguments with other members of your household?

Bear in mind that even books which are no longer on sale in traditional outlets such as high street bookshops can still be bought elsewhere. Indeed, the internet opens up myriad opportunities to find even rare items through online sellers or specialist sites.

Future generations might want them

Whether or not you have children of your own, you may wish to leave your most treasured books as part of your legacy. But who exactly will you give them to? Do you have particular relatives in mind? If one of your grandchildren is fascinated by military history it might make sense to keep your RAF history collection. If a niece is applying to study literature at university, perhaps she might want some of your hardback classics. Why not gift them now so that you can witness the pleasure they'll bring?

Don't be disappointed however if your books aren't regarded with the same affection by the friends or relatives to whom you bestow them.

If you're holding on to reference books note that they are no longer the indispensable sources of information they once were. I recall visiting the local public library in my childhood to trawl through leather-bound encyclopaedia. Nowadays, even primary school children conduct research online.

They're part of a set

Do you own a complete set of Dickens or boxed sets of paperbacks? Clients often say that they feel obliged to keep the entire collection intact even if it's taking up valuable shelf space.

If you enjoyed one volume of a set but haven't got around to reading the rest, set a time limit after which you'll think again about keeping them. Maybe put the set on the 'to-read' shelf (see "I'll read them soon"). There's no need to keep them indefinitely.

Don't feel inhibited or guilty about breaking up a set. If you want to keep one volume, it's perfectly permissible to give away the rest.

Finally, is it possible that you're not reading the remaining books because the print is so small or the book is too heavy or unwieldy? These are common problems with anthologies or 'complete works' and if that's the case is there really a good reason to keep them?

They remind me of my childhood

I've kept a selection of Ladybird books out of nostalgia but all the bird-watching manuals and joke books have long gone to charity shop heaven. It's gratifying to know that other children will read them. If there are books which you can't part with because they bring back childhood memories, you might like to store them in a memory box. On the other hand, if you keep a few on display, there's still some chance you may pick them up and peruse them in the future. As with other forms of clutter, be selective so you can find and enjoy your belongings; if you keep too many, the ones you value the most are likely to be overlooked.

It's good for my kids to see books in the home

No doubt books reflect family interests but if there are too many of them stacked on shelves and surfaces your younger readers are likely to be as overwhelmed as you are. They may find it difficult to make choices when there are too many options.

One of my clients was anxious that her ten year-old son had stopped reading despite the vast number of books in his bedroom. We packed up all the books, leaving just half a dozen select titles on the shelf and hey presto, he picked one up the next day.

It's quality not quantity which will inspire them

Children's reading habits vary but in my opinion it's quality not quantity which will inspire them. And ultimately, they are more likely to be motivated to pick up books if they see you reading books rather than just buying them.

Paper

Why do piles of paper become such a problem? At first glance paper appears so innocuous – each sheet so light and flimsy, each envelope so slim and portable – but it streams silently into our homes, spreads surreptitiously over surfaces and then takes root. No sooner do you clear one pile than more arrives, like those self-lighting birthday candles which relight as soon as you blow them out.

It's terrifying

I've yet to meet anyone diagnosed with papyrophobia, an aversion to touching any kind of paper or irrational fear of being injured by it. But if you're too scared to sort through unopened post or to clear out old newspapers, you're not alone. Many of the clients I've helped in recent years have described paperwork as the stuff of nightmares.

Here are some tips to help you overcome your fear:

* **Name it**

    What exactly are you afraid of? Chances are it's

not the paper itself but rather thoughts associated with it. Are you worried about what you might unearth? Are you afraid of being swamped by decisions? Or perhaps what intimidates you is the thought of what happens next, after you finish decluttering. Fear of success can be just as debilitating as fear of failure. If you can identify and articulate specific concerns, it will be easier to manage them

- **Navigate it**

  Now try to confront those fears and assess the risks – how likely are those negative outcomes? And if they did materialise, how would you cope? Once you start to dissect the worst-case scenarios you may realise that you have the resources or strengths to deal with them or that they are not quite as bad as you imagined. Remember that the story you're telling yourself is just one perspective and it's always possible to look at a situation from a different view point. It might also help to share your anxieties with someone else

- **Nail it**

  As Susan Jeffers, author of the self-help classic Feel the Fear and Do It Anyway says, 'The only way to get rid of the fear of doing something is to go out and … do it!'[20] Stop procrastinating and identify the very first tasks to tackle. Hold onto the vision of what you're trying to achieve – for instance a clear desk or dining room – but take small steps towards your goal

Dealing with paperwork can seem insurmountable because of the scale of the project. Breaking it into chunks can make it all the more manageable. Sort through just one pile of papers or clear one single surface then celebrate your victory in the battle against paper clutter. Once you get started, you're bound to realise that the fear was worse than the reality.

You might also want to read "I'm afraid of what I might find".

I don't know what to do

You're motivated and ready, you've set time aside to declutter but now what? Here's a simple action plan:

---

20   Susan Jeffers, *Feel The Fear And Do It Anyway: How to Turn Your Fear and Indecision into Confidence and Action*, Vermilion, 2007

- **Gather**

    Collect all the papers from different rooms and take them to a designated sorting station, such as a kitchen table. Use a laundry basket or large plastic box to contain and control it. Continue to transfer paper from around the house to your sorting station until it's done

- **Sort**

    Divide and rule papers by sorting into broad categories such as personal, financial, house, car and children. Gather unopened post together and then open it all in one go. Sort letters from the same person or organisation into piles. Tackle each batch in turn rather than shifting attention from bank statements to school reports to invoices. Don't try to make too many decisions at the same time – jumping from one set of issues to another can be very taxing

- **Reduce**

    Let go of paper which no longer serves a purpose. Set up large bags or bins for recycling or shredding before you get started. Toss envelopes directly into recycling, together with old newspapers, magazines, journals, packaging and circulars. To safeguard your privacy and protect against identity theft I advise you to shred any documents which show your personal data. Invest in a good shredder of your own or find a local company to do it for you

* **Organise**

    It's important to find a way to store and organise paper which works for you. There's no need to spend a fortune on sophisticated filing systems or stylish stationery. There are plenty of cheap and cheerful storage solutions. I like to use transparent files, clearly labelled, so that contents can be seen at a glance. See also "I don't know how to store paperwork"

* **Maintain**

    Devise and practise routines to keep clutter at bay in the future – see more on this in "Next Steps" at the end of this book. It takes time to create new habits so don't despair if you occasionally relapse

Feel free to adapt or amend this to suit your own situation but you should be able to use this as a template. Decluttering isn't rocket science but it does entail a range of different activities and without planning it's easy to get overwhelmed. Attempting to tackle these tasks concurrently can also lead to even more chaos and confusion so try to take them one at a time.

I don't know what to keep

While there are very real and concrete reasons for keeping certain documents, you don't need to retain everything. After all, if you can't lay your hands on vital documents because they're buried in a mire of superfluous stuff, you might just as well not own it anyway.

If you're self-employed, consult your bookkeeper or accountant to find out how many years of records you need to keep. If you have savings or investments, a financial adviser can suggest how many statements to keep. There is no shame in not knowing and if you've sought out professional help you can be confident in disposing of the papers which fall outside of their recommended datelines. Once you're established the parameters of your paper archive, you can look forward to disposing of batches every year.

I don't know how to store paperwork

What this usually means is that you don't have systems for what to keep and where to keep it. If these systems are simple enough, you'll be able to streamline your paperwork and keep it under control. The benefits of this are great. As organiser Rivka Caroline says it often takes more effort to be disorganised than to be organised.[21]

As noted before, it's impossible to organise anything when there's too much of it. So aim to declutter first (see "I don't know what to do"). Then you might like to organise in terms of three different time frames:

- **Archive**

  Records, souvenirs and documents belonging to the past but which may still be needed. These don't need to be stored in prime locations such as desks but could be filed in a cabinet or stored in boxes, perhaps on higher shelves or up in an attic

- **Current usage**

  Documents you refer to now such as school newsletters, event listings and gym schedules. Do you need these on display, such as stuck on your fridge or noticeboard? Store others where they can be found quickly and easily. Group them according to theme and use boxes, baskets or trays to stop them spreading

---

21   Rivka Caroline, *From Frazzled to Focused: The Ultimate Guide for Moms Who Want to Reclaim Their Time, Their Sanity and Their Lives*, River Grove Books, 2013

- **Future**

  Anything you don't need right now but might in the future, such as information about possible holiday destinations, health practitioners or home maintenance companies. Keep the papers in marked folders or in one basket or tray. If you catch yourself holding on to paper 'just in case' think twice about how it's likely to contribute to clutter

Finally, here are some tips on how best to store your paper:

- Store folders vertically, not horizontally. They are less likely to be lost or overlooked
- Designate a particular place for key documents
- Don't trust your memory: compile a master list so that you can locate files when you need them

You might also find "I'm naturally disorganised" helpful.

I'm afraid of what I might find

Are you afraid of what you might encounter when you open the post or start rummaging through long-abandoned papers?

These are the most common fears I hear from clients:

- **Debt**

  Unpaid bills or neglected bank statements can be painful reminders of a precarious financial situation. The irony is that clutter can be both a cause and a consequence of anxiety, especially about money. If you're worried about debt, contact your local branch of the Citizens Advice Bureau for free, expert advice[22]

- **Relationship breakdowns**

  Correspondence and documents might relate to disputes, divorce or incidents which evoke complex emotional responses. One client was reluctant to clear clutter from her desk because she couldn't face the possibility of finding letters from her parents who had both died in recent months

- **Memories**

  Even happy memories can be difficult to process at times. You may not feel that you want to dedicate the time to reading old diaries or love letters – but it may be too difficult to resist. If you know that sorting through shoe boxes of papers is likely to

---

22   *https://www.citizensadvice.org.uk*

draw you back into the past, you may prefer to delay this task

Tackling your fear or worries will ultimately result in less stress and worry, and you'll feel more in control for the future, so it's worth taking a deep breath and taking that first step.

I'm wary of paperless systems

It's possible to reduce the quantity of paper entering your home by switching to paperless billing and online communications. Nowadays it's perfectly acceptable to pay bills online, bank online and send out invitations by email.

Consider the benefits of this: less paper being used leading to fewer trees being felled, less time spent storing documentation, easy access to information online and potential discounts for online billing.

You may be wary of paperless systems but at some point they will be the only systems available – modern communication is moving away from paper and post. If you're not entirely confident, maybe try switching just one account at a time. Or ask if you can opt for paperless billing on a trial basis for a limited time period.

I don't deal with it regularly

If you have long working days or if you're juggling lots of commitments chances are that you won't want to start organising paperwork when you have spare time, and it will become less and less appealing if you don't tackle it regularly.

To make dealing with paper as pain free as possible, set up routines which require minimal effort. If you can spend five minutes twice daily on cleaning your teeth without even thinking about it, you can also master the skill of opening your post once a day.

Make it as easy as possible to recycle unwanted paper. If you have to walk too far to discard it, you're less likely to do it. One client found that by placing a small basket under the table in her hallway, she could throw away envelopes, circulars and junk as soon as post arrived. When the basket was full she emptied it into a recycling bin – a simple but effective clutter-busting habit.

Identify tasks to do at different intervals:

- Daily – Open post, recycle envelopes and junk mail
- Weekly – Recycle old newspapers and magazines
- Monthly – Check and file bills and invoices
- Annually – Prepare paperwork for tax return

Once you create a schedule like this, you won't have to think about when to complete certain tasks. Keep routines as simple as possible so that you're more likely to stick to them.

There's no space in my filing cabinet

Do you have a filing cabinet that's stuffed so full of paper that you can barely open it, let alone find the things you need?

Is it really a lack of space or too much superfluous paper? At some point you'll need to empty the unit altogether and be prepared to cull anything which no longer serves a purpose. Look out in particular for empty folders, duplicated documents, outdated newsletters and paper which is decades old.

In addition to clutter you might find some surprises. One client had been in the habit of tossing loose change into the cabinet in her home study. When we tipped out the drawers she discovered coins adding up to three hundred pounds. Just imagine what you might find!

I'm worried about identity theft

Are you reluctant to let go of paper which contains personal data? Invest in a decent shredder. I don't usually encourage clients to buy anything (who needs more stuff?) but a good quality shredder is a worthwhile investment.

Check whether shredded paper can be recycled in your area. If not, it could be used for animal bedding.

The Kitchen

We spend a lot of time in our kitchens – cooking, eating, entertaining, working, studying – so it's not surprising that clutter builds up there. And perhaps because kitchens are so often the hub of a home, the impact of clutter can be far-reaching. A recent study showed, for example, that people who ate in cluttered kitchens tended to snack more frequently and chose less healthy food options.[23] So a tidy kitchen will have lots of benefits.

Estate agents tell me that prospective buyers scrutinise kitchens more than any other room so if you plan to sell your home that's all the more reason to keep your kitchen free of clutter.

I might need lots of glasses

Whiskey tumblers, martini glasses, sherry schooners – why not streamline by opting for only the most generic

---

23   Lenny R. Vartanian, Kristin M. Kernan, Brian Wansink, *Clutter, Chaos and Overconsumption: The Role of Mindset in Stressful and Chaotic Food Environments*, http://journals.sagepub.com/doi/abs/10.1177/0013916516628178

types? Declutter and donate the rest. Unless you're a wine lover, you could even get away with just using tumblers – they're easier to stack and clean too.

What to do with the mismatched array of drinking glasses you've accumulated over the years? Your collection might include some of the following:

* Anything scratched or foggy – glass can become stained by minerals in water or etched if regularly washed in a dishwasher. Try soaking them in vinegar for a few minutes and then wipe off any marks. If that doesn't help the damage is likely to be permanent so recycle them

* Garishly-coloured shot glasses, embellished with slogans in a language you don't understand, souvenirs of nights out in far-off countries – raise a toast to good times and then let them go

* An over-sized beer glass which was once full of sweets, a prize which you or your child won at a school fair – a fun gimmick but you've never used the glass so let it go

* A pair of cocktail glasses and perhaps an unused shaker and matching ice bucket – impulse buys, perhaps after taking a mixology course. If they are

not regularly used give them away so that someone else can make better use of them

- Assorted wine glasses of varying shapes and sizes. Wine merchants and some supermarkets will loan glassware (often at no cost) so even if you're in the habit of organising parties there's really no need to keep so many

I might find the lids

Is there a drawer in your kitchen stuffed full of boxes without lids, and lids without boxes? The mystery of the unmatched container is one which plagues many homes. Taming the Tupperware drawer can be one of the most tiresome tasks when you set out to declutter the kitchen.

Gather all the containers, match up the boxes and lids and stack them in groups. Decide which ones you would buy again if you were starting from scratch. As for the unmatched items, put all the singletons in a large box with a dated label. Whenever you come across a spare box or lid try to reunite it with its missing mate. After a certain period (three months, say) consider recycling the items which remain in the box or find other uses for them which don't require lids. For example, they could stand in your fridge or pantry or bathroom/kitchen cabinet to keep small items together.

A few more words about plastic tableware: if your children are old enough to drink from a glass, and certainly if they have left home, you don't need to keep all those tumblers or plastic plates.

I don't need them anymore but still can't let them go

Clutter represents memories of the past as well as aspirations for the future and that often makes letting go of belongings difficult. And this can be particularly true if you're going through divorce, downsizing or bereavement. The best advice I can offer in these situations is not to rush your decisions or your actions, but rather to take time to acknowledge any difficult feelings which arise.

Here's an example to illustrate what I mean:

At the age of seventy-five, Katerina was downsizing from a large family home to a compact flat. While looking forward to living in a smaller, more modern home she was finding it difficult to make decisions about what to take with her. Crockery was a huge challenge. Katerina opened cabinets where shelves were stacked neatly with dozens of colourful plates, bowls and serving dishes. She explained that for the last twenty years she had rented out rooms and provided meals to foreign students. She enjoyed their company and maintained contact with many for years afterwards. Letting go of crockery was a painful admission that that phase of her life was ending and she worried about being lonely in her new home.

If you're finding it difficult to part from things, ask yourself what they represent. Change is obviously unsettling and decluttering can evoke painful emotions associated with loss. One of the best way to come to terms with these feelings is to talk about them with a sympathetic friend.

One day I'll make my own bread/pasta/ice cream/ popcorn/yoghurt

Did you buy yourself a shiny new appliance? Perhaps you were enticed by the idea of waking up to fresh, home-baked rolls for breakfast or the thought of enjoying homemade popcorn or pasta. Or maybe you received it gleefully as a gift. No matter how it arrived in your kitchen it only deserves to stay if you do in fact use it.

It only deserves to stay if you do in fact use it

I have a 'size matters' principle: the larger the item the more it has to justify its continued existence in your home. It's also worth considering how essential these appliances really are. For centuries people baked bread without bread makers and there are plenty of recipes available which don't require one.

Bread makers, ice cream machines, pasta makers, popcorn makers should all come with a warning: 'Please enjoy this product. But if you haven't taken it out of the box within six months or have only used it occasionally, don't feel compelled to keep it'.

If you're determined to hold onto a specific appliance think about where you will store it. If it stays on the worktop will you be more inclined to use it in the future? Or perhaps it could be relegated to a cupboard? There's a danger that it may become 'out of sight, out of mind' but perhaps it would help to grant it a temporary reprieve. Write the date on which you last used it on a post-it note or sticker and declutter the cupboard within six months. If you haven't used your gadget by then it's probably time to let it go.

Some charity shops such as the British Heart Foundation accept small electrical items.[24] Otherwise advertise and give them away via local newspaper listings or Facebook groups.

I might use all the free stuff

Have you acquired a collection of unused chopsticks, sachets of ketchup or soy sauce, plastic cutlery or serviettes which arrived with takeaways?

It's possible you might need some but it's unlikely you'll need *all* of them. Are you planning to host a themed outdoor picnic for dozens of friends? If not, it makes sense to recycle them.

Check the 'use by' dates of sachets and discard those which are past their prime.

Finally, take pre-emptive action. Next time you order food to be delivered, tell the restaurant in advance that you don't need any more cutlery or condiments.

---

24   https://www.bhf.org.uk/shop/donating-goods

I can't get rid of my mugs

According to the Guinness Book of Records, the largest collection of mugs owned by one individual was 6,352 (belonging to an American called Bob Caldwell). You might find it reassuring to know that someone else owns more mugs than you do!

But if your shelves are groaning, maybe it's time to give them a health check.

- Chipped or cracked mugs – will you ever get around to repairing them?
- Mug shots – mugs with photos of your children or grandchildren which you don't like to use because you're afraid they'll get damaged. Find somewhere else to display them, ideally where they can serve a purpose, perhaps on your desk as a pencil holder
- Travel souvenirs or gifts – do they hold special memories? Do you really need the mug to remember the holiday or the friend?
- Awkwardly shaped mugs, perhaps with scratchy rims you don't enjoy using – would you really miss them?

Finally, while many mugs are special, some are likely to be more special than others. Pick out the ones which delight you and donate the rest to a charity shop or to people who will love them more than you do.

I can't give away my wedding presents

The short answer to this is: yes, you can. That cappuccino machine or decorative vase or block of knives was presented to you with love. But you don't have to keep it forever. My view is that when you're given a gift you're also given a choice: to keep it or not.

I've visited more than one kitchen replete with unopened wedding gifts, sometimes years or even decades after the event. If you haven't used them or no longer want them, it's fine to re-gift them (ideally not to the friends who gave them to you in the first place!) or sell them and buy yourself something else. Alternatively, donate them to charity and enable others to benefit from them.

I'm saving it for when my children set up home

If your offspring are about to set up a home of their own, even if only temporarily, they might appreciate some extra dinner plates. But if your children are still in primary school, you may want to think again.

How long do you want to keep saucepans on the

off-chance that your children might make use of them? If you decide to keep them, pack them up in a labelled box and store them elsewhere such as in a garage or shed. Bear in mind that basic kitchenware is relatively inexpensive nowadays, and youngsters may prefer to choose their own.

I might need those cleaning products

If there's one space in your kitchen that's likely to be cluttered, it's under the sink. If yours is crammed with dozens of different disinfectants, detergents, sprays and sanitisers a stock-take is probably long overdue. While you may need *some* of the products you've accumulated it's unlikely that you need them all.

The best approach is to empty out the entire cupboard, put everything on the kitchen table or worktop and take a long, hard look.

The following items can probably be decluttered:

* Rubber gloves which are past their prime
* Carrier bags – how many are you likely to use?
* Anything musty, dusty or mouldy such as old dishcloths

- Cleaning fluids which are out of date
- Over-sized bags for bins which you no longer own
- Coloured pegs which you no longer use to hang laundry
- Products which are almost empty – can you combine them?
- Laundry products – if you haven't used them because you don't like the smell, don't keep them
- Bits and pieces which once belonged to gadgets you no longer own

Where possible dispose of things ethically by recycling. Although charity shops can't resell them, they might accept them to clean their offices.

Where possible dispose of things ethically

One of the reasons that kitchen cleaning materials have multiplied in recent years is the advent of super-specialised products. If space is limited, why not try switching to multi-purpose cleaning products? You'll find that in most cases they are just as effective.

In the future, try not to let products accumulate. If you've bought in bulk to save money or 'just in case' you run out, resolve to use up some of your stocks before replenishing them.

The Bathroom

Possibly the smallest room in the house and probably the one with the least built-in storage, your bathroom is particularly prone to clutter because of the wide range of products and paraphernalia used there.

However keeping bathroom clutter under control makes it easier to clean surfaces and creates a calmer and more relaxing atmosphere. You'll be able to find toiletries or medications when you need them and will avoid spending money on things you already own.

I'll use the miniatures one day

Are your bathroom cabinets full of travel-size lotions from hotels? Or sample sachets which came glued to the front of magazines? When you sort them into categories – shower gel, shampoo, conditioner – you might be shocked by the quantity.

Discard anything which looks or smells grungy, unappealing or past its best. Like cosmetics, liquid products can turn rancid or cause allergic reactions.

Then think critically about reducing the remaining stash. Consider each set of products in turn. Ask not 'do

I need this?' but rather 'when will I use it?'

* **Camping or travelling**
  Keep a handful of basic products, if you will. But even if you're planning to backpack around the world, you'll only need a few supplies

* **Play time**
  If you have young children, you might wish to keep a few plastic bottles for them to play with in the bath. Then again, do they already have a surfeit of bath clutter?

* **After exercise or sport**
  Pop a few of the products you're most likely to use in your gym bag. But again, be selective in terms of quality and quantity

* **Guests**
  Do you run a bed and breakfast or host overnight visitors on a regular basis? If not, perhaps you don't need quite so many toiletries?

Alternatively, pack up the miniatures and donate them to charities such as local hospices or homeless shelters. And finally, next time you stay in a hotel, resist the temptation to bring home more toiletries.

I never throw out old toothbrushes

When I help clients to declutter bathrooms, the one item I'm almost certain to encounter at the back of a cabinet is an old toothbrush, or maybe two or three....

The British Dental Journal reported that toothbrushes can accumulate as many as ten billion bacteria.[25] No wonder dentists recommend changing your toothbrush every three months. But what to do with an old toothbrush when you replace it?

Until recently, plastic brushes with nylon bristles were notoriously difficult to recycle but an increasing number of dental hygiene products are manufactured from recycled and recyclable materials. If you're concerned about the environmental impact of throwing away your old toothbrush check packaging when you buy a new one to ensure that it can be disposed of responsibly when the time comes. Alternatively, look out for biodegradable products.

Old toothbrushes can be used for countless tasks, including scrubbing bathroom tiles, bringing a gleam to jewellery, cleaning computer keyboards or shining shoes. But if you do keep your toothbrush for any of these reasons store it with your cleaning products, not in the bathroom!

---

25   https://www.nature.com/articles/sj.bdj.2016.503

I like buying in bulk

Are your cabinets crammed with multi-packs of soaps? When you loaded up the trolley with over-sized packages of toilet paper or six-packs of shampoo you probably didn't think about the clutter they would create.

If mega-packs are causing mayhem in your bathroom, here are some tips:

- Establish an embargo. Don't buy more stuff until you've used up some of the existing cache
- Practise saying to yourself 'I have enough' while shopping. Don't be seduced by special offers
- If you're tempted to buy in bulk while shopping online, visualise the space available to store stuff or better still, pop into the bathroom and remind yourself what you already own. Check out existing supplies before checking out more clutter!
- Finally, if you can't resist buying multi-packs arrange to split your purchases with a friend or neighbour

Remember that nowadays you can buy almost anything online even at short notice so there's less need to keep large stocks.

It was a gift

Shelf and cabinet space in your bathroom is likely to be quite limited so there's no point keeping products you don't intend to use. Have you been given expensive spa products, gift-boxed soaps or lotions whose scents you don't like? The person who gave them to you need never know if you exercise your right to declutter. Gift sets or unopened products can be sold online or donated as prizes to a charity event such as a school fair. Alternatively, take them all to your local shelter for homeless people.

> There's no point keeping products you don't intend to use

You can appreciate the kindness of friends or relatives who've given you these items without feeling obliged to keep them.

I might need those medicines

Medicine cabinets and first aid boxes are often clutter magnets.

Here are some tips on how to clear the clutter:

- Take unused prescription drugs to a pharmacy who will dispose of them safely. Don't flush them down the toilet or sink because they risk entering the water supply
- Check use-by dates on medicines and pills – they may no longer be effective
- Batteries can run out in devices such as TENS machines or electronic thermometers so check that these are in good working order
- Check the expiry dates of sun creams and discard those which are past their best
- Discard old plasters which have lost their adhesive
- Grungy bandages can be refreshed in the laundry but don't keep more than you really need

It's worth doing this at least once a year so that you can find essential medicines if and when you need them.

Technology & Entertainment

The rapid pace of technological change has transformed every aspect of our lives, including home entertainment. Thanks to the popularity of streaming sites, for example, we no longer need to buy physical objects – videos, CDs, DVDs – to watch films or listen to music but many of us struggle to let go of these familiar items.

From headsets to hand-held devices, we're also holding onto outdated phones and related accessories. In 2016 93% of adults in the UK owned or used a mobile phone and the average time between upgrades was just twenty-six months. No wonder tech clutter is on the rise. [26]

I might need those old phones

When you upgrade your mobile phone, do you hold onto the old handset, 'just in case'? And what happens to the cables, chargers and other unidentifiable

---

26   *https://www.ofcom.org.uk/about-ofcom/latest/media/facts*

whatnots which come in the box?

If yours is one of the estimated twenty million outdated handsets which clutter up UK homes, why not find a smart way to dispose of it? Check online for charities who will recycle phones or reuse them and even if the phone is discontinued you may still be able to sell it.

I keep old cables and chargers

As for the cables and chargers, if you no longer have the device for which they were designed is there any point in keeping them? Perhaps if you run a guesthouse, there might be some justification – those extra chargers might be appreciated by guests who forget to bring their own. Otherwise, it's hard to imagine when you might possibly need them.

I don't know what to do with old media

Sales of audio cassettes (or 'tapes' as we called them in the 1980s!) were already in rapid decline in 2007 when a BBC report estimated that five hundred million could be found in British homes. A decade later, many of those relics are still contributing to household clutter. In addition, you've probably accumulated a host of videos, CDs and DVDs.

Here are some questions to guide you towards making decisions about your collection:

* Do you still own a working device on which to play them? If you don't possess a 'boom box' or cassette player on your hi-fi system and your Sony Walkman has long since vanished how are you ever going to listen to those audio cassettes? And if you no longer own a VCR there's no point in keeping video cassettes

* Are your devices compatible? Even if you still possess a functioning VCR, can it be connected to your current television or computer? Do you have all the necessary cables and, perhaps more importantly, sufficient know-how to rig it all up?

* Assuming that you do have the technological means to play your 1980s music or films, can you count on quality of sound and vision? Do you have other more appealing ways to listen to music or watch films at home?

● Be honest, how much time do you currently have to listen to music or watch films, and when you do make time, how often do you choose to listen to old favourites rather than discover new ones?

Don't hang onto obsolete tech in the hope that future generations might want it. With the exception of vinyl they probably won't. If you want to use artefacts from your youth to educate others about the past, perhaps keep just a very small selection to show them.

I'd advise you not to spend time trying to sell your old media. Clients and colleagues who have tried to sell these items online report limited success. However most charity shops will accept DVDs and CDs and you could try giving them away on Freegle, Freecycle or local community groups' social media pages.[27] There are very few opportunities in the UK to recycle audio or video cassettes but packaging and plastic cases might be recyclable – check with your local recycling centre.

---

27   *https://my.freecycle.org, https://www.ilovefreegle.org*

Toys

Parents in the UK are the world's second biggest spenders on toys for their children.[28] From babies to teenagers, as children grow older, the number and range of playthings proliferates. No wonder so many parents and carers feel that their homes are overrun by toys. This not only encroaches on the physical space available to rest, play or entertain; it also contributes to tensions between family members and heightens stress.

It's your presence, not your presents which matters most

Oliver James, psychologist and author of Love Bombing, suggests that, instead of showering children with gifts, parents should share experiences such as holidays which children will remember. It's your presence, not your presents which matters most.[29]

Meanwhile decluttering skills are life skills too so it's worth involving children in the process from an early age. Learning to make decisions, letting go of things

28   The top spenders are in Australia – http://www.telegraph.co.uk/finance/newsbysector/retailandconsumer/11624459/The-UK-has-the-worlds-second-highest-spend-per-child-on-toys.html
29   Oliver James, Love Bombing: Reset your Child's Emotional Thermostat, Karnac, 2012

they no longer need or love, finding ways to reuse or recycle, and most of all, developing routines which help to control clutter – these are all useful activities for children to learn while they're young.

My children need lots of choice

I'm all for offering *some* choice – children need to learn how to make decisions, after all. But too many options are overwhelming and unnecessary. Cut down on clutter by reducing the range of toys on display at any one time. You might like to pack some of the toys away and rotate them on a weekly or monthly basis, which would offer some degree of novelty. Alternatively limit the toys to just a few of each category – if you have multiple jigsaws or board games be realistic about how many can be used at one time and put away the others.

Visitors might enjoy them

If you regularly have young visitors you may feel a need to provide them with entertainment. You may have kept toys treasured by your own children when they were young or perhaps you've created a collection specifically for friends' children. If they're tucked away tidily in a place where they don't bother you, that's fine. But if they're taking up precious space or creating obstacles in your lounge, maybe it's time to relocate them.

How often do you expect young visitors? If it's only once a year, the toys could be stored in the loft or garage instead of cluttering up space you need for other things. But do you really need such a wide range? Two or three stuffed animals might suffice instead of twenty? Opt for things which will appeal to various ages such as coloured pens and pencils. Lego is popular with all age groups, but again, no need to keep vast amounts.

Do you really need such a wide range?

My child won't give anything away

Children don't generally like the idea of 'getting rid' of anything and can be possessive about their belongings but here are some suggestions for teaching them decluttering habits:

- Set positive goals and explain how they will benefit. For instance, rather than moaning about a messy floor, put on some music and talk to them about making room to dance. In other words, help them to visualise direct and tangible benefits to creating a clutter-free space

- Explain that everything comes into our lives for a reason but that we don't need to keep everything forever. Show respect for their belongings: don't talk about 'chucking things out' but help them to appreciate if new toys and games keep flowing into your home, some will have to leave

- Adopt a particular charity as a family project and explain how donated toys help to raise money for animals or children who are unwell, for example. Some charities encourage children to sign up to special schemes, including newsletters[30]

- Suggest selling old toys or games online or at a car boot or yard sale. Children might enjoy 'setting up shop' as well as earning some money (see my tips on selling online and car boot sales in "Next Steps")

---

30   For example, the PDSA which provides free vet services runs a Pet Protectors Club for youngsters http://www.petprotectors.org.uk

Remember that it takes time and patience to shift habits but try to establish routines with your children. The more often you encourage them to review and organise their toys, the more likely they are to develop decision-making skills and decluttering habits.

Guide children to make decisions but don't pressure. Point out duplicates or games they no longer play with. Demonstrate your own commitment to decluttering. When children witness your delight at creating space and order, they're bound to be motivated by your example.

Next Steps

Disposal strategies

Now that you are ready to start decluttering, let's talk about the best strategies for disposing of the things which you decide you no longer want or need.

Minimising your contribution to landfill

There are plenty of eco-friendly ways to declutter:

- Find out where your local recycling centre is and check what they are willing to accept. Most will accept small electrical items, paper, glass, metals, cardboard and paints

- Household goods can be donated to community reuse projects, but if you take your donations along in person, resist the temptation to bring home anything donated by others[31]

- Art supplies and craft materials can be given away

---

31   Check out roadshows run by the Furniture Re-Use Network - http://www.frn.org.uk

to local schools, nurseries, community groups or perhaps to people in your neighbourhood with similar hobbies or interests. Post notices on sites such as Freecyle or Freegle, or search for local community groups on Facebook[32]

- Take part in book-sharing projects such as the schemes run by Book Crossing or Book Fairies.[33] Or leave your book in designated public places such as waiting rooms at stations

- Many supermarkets have battery disposal facilities

Finally, it's always worth searching the internet for organisations who might be looking for more unusual items.

Donating to charity

Check the websites of high street charities to find out what goods they'll accept. Many can arrange collection from your home. With local groups on Facebook and apps promoting community projects, it's not difficult to

---

32   *https://my.freecycle.org, https://www.ilovefreegle.org*
33   *http://www.bookcrossing.com, https://ibelieveinbookfairies.com*

find a worthy cause. For instance:

- Old blankets and towels, even ones which are shabby, can be donated to animal rescue shelters
- Warm winter clothes such as coats, scarves, hats can be taken to homeless shelters
- Food which is still in date can be taken to a food bank
- Children's toys and games can be donated to a hospital or hospice
- Furniture and working household items can be offered to larger charities such as the British Heart Foundation or Sue Ryder, or redistributed via the Furniture Donation Network[34]
- Magazines and books might be welcomed by care homes or your GP surgery

A growing number of apps can help you to find ways to donate to local charities. For instance, Olio was started to combat food waste but has been now expanded to help recycle household items, which can be listed with a request for a 'pay as your feel' donation.[35] Gone for Good also helps to match decluttered items with local charities.[36]

---

*34   https://www.bhf.org.uk/shop/donating-goods, http://www.
sueryder.org/shop-with-us/donate-to-our-shops, https://www.
furnituredonationnetwork.org*
35   https://olioex.com
36   https://goneforgood.org.uk

I once helped to declutter a hundred tiny flowerpots which had been lovingly filled with plastic flowers by an expert flower arranger. I took them to a local care home, just before Rosh Hashana (Jewish New Year) and they were given as gifts to the residents to mark the holiday. With a little imagination you could find a new home for the most unlikely items.

Car boot sales

Personally I'm not a fan of car boot sales but if you fancy giving it a try here are some tips:

- Research the events in your area and ask around to find out which ones are recommended
- Enlist the help of a friend or family member. You will really need another pair of hands
- Sort your stuff in advance so that it's quick and easy to load and unload
- Arrive early, preferably an hour before the event starts. Seasoned sellers will queue before the gates open and then dash to grab the best pitch
- Take plenty of loose change and make a note of how much cash is in your 'float'

- Wear comfortable and sturdy footwear because you'll be on your feet for hours
- A body belt will be handy for change and car keys
- Keep your phone and other valuables out of sight, ideally locked away in your car
- Be prepared for haggling and try not to be insulted if you're offered silly prices for things you once held dear or believe to be more valuable
- Take a flask and snacks so that you don't have to leave your pitch (or be dependent on junk food vans)
- Plan what to do at the end of the day with anything which hasn't sold. My suggestion is to make a beeline for the nearest charity shop and donate everything to a worthy cause so that you don't take it home again

A golden rule for attending car boot sales is not to buy anyone else's clutter! Remember that the point of the exercise is to make money while decluttering, not to acquire more stuff!

For details of local boot sales as well as some more handy tips, you might like to visit Car Boot Junction's website.[37]

---

37   http://www.carbootjunction.com

Selling online

If you're keen to sell your unwanted items online take time to figure out the logistics and ensure that you understand the terms and conditions as well as the technology.

Here are some tips:

* For platforms such as eBay, download the app and read the advice for sellers
* Research the market by looking at listings of similar items, both current and completed
* Think about the keywords which potential buyers would use to search for your items and include these in your listings
* Take good quality, clear photographs – these can really make a difference
* If you're aiming for a quick sale, opt for 'buy-it-now' listings
* To maximise the price, set up an auction
* eBay enables you to donate a proportion of the final sale price to a registered charity so you can share your profits if you choose

Don't forget to factor in postage, packaging, commission charges and the cost of travel to and from the post office. And don't underestimate your most valuable resource – your time.

You might also want to try low-tech options such as noticeboards in libraries, newsagents or supermarkets.

Don't underestimate your most valuable resource – your time

Keeping a collection together

If you dedicated time, money and effort into building up a collection of specialist items it may be hard to envisage separating them. From hand-carved chess sets to cabinets of salt-and-pepper shakers from around the world, collections express personal tastes and preferences; they reflect years of curation, bringing together disparate items and creating something more significant than the sum of its parts. Perhaps the most unusual collection I've encountered in a private home was five hundred police batons, laid out on the carpet of a spare bedroom, all neatly ordered and catalogued.

Consider contacting specialist dealers or websites who may be able to advertise the collection for sale as a whole, or donate it to charity with the stipulation that it remains together.

Finally, you might like to document the collection by photographing it before you say goodbye to it.

A memory box

Throughout this book I've mentioned that you might like to save a few select keepsakes, and you might want to create a memory box for these. If you have children or grandchildren you might want to create one for them too. Choose a good quality, sturdy box with a lid so that you can count on it to store your items safely for the future and then store it out of sight. You might want to use a decorative container but a plastic box will do the job just as well.

Self-storage

A by-product of our consumer society is the rapid growth of the self-storage industry: warehouses offering customers lockable units of varying sizes. Like many professional organisers, I'm not a fan of off-site storage but concede that it's useful in certain circumstances such as:

- Temporary relocation such as moving abroad for a specific period
- Property sale or rental, to improve the appearance of your home while selling or to accommodate tenants who don't need your furniture
- Renovation or decorating work, for items which might otherwise be damaged
- Between rentals, for instance students vacating rented accommodation during holidays
- Separation and divorce, to store belongings while temporarily living in a smaller home

These temporary situations all involve considerable physical and emotional upheaval so paying for off-site storage can alleviate stress and anxiety but the key is to remember that it is a *temporary* solution. For many people these facilities provide an opportunity to accumulate clutter. The cost of self-storage adds up over time, so before you pay for it ask yourself whether you're planning to store things you no longer need, use or value.

Preventing future clutter

As with all strategies for change, it's not just the initial results which matter but maintenance too.

Once you start to experience the joys of decluttering, you'll become attuned to ways of preventing further build-up. Here are some suggestions to keep clutter at bay:

* **Shop more mindfully**

   Notice how your mood affects what, when, how and how much you buy. Are you more likely to buy things which you don't really need if you shop when tired, lonely or bored for example? Steel yourself against promotions of 'must-have' items and learn to resist special offers and flash sales

* **Reject fads and fashions**

   As you sort through your wardrobe, take time to figure out what shapes, colours and styles suit you best. This will help you to shop more judiciously in the future. There's no harm in experimenting with new looks but you're less likely to end up with clothes you don't wear if you understand what makes you look and feel great

- **Create traditions**
  Devise routines to declutter at set times of the year so that family members anticipate and join in. For example, you could encourage your children to sort out toys and donate a certain proportion to charity before each birthday or festival

- **Review your gift policy**
  Prior to special occasions or seasonal celebrations remind friends and family of your mission to avoid clutter. Explain that shared experiences would mean more than more scented candles or woolly sweaters; set an example by giving vouchers for meals out, day trips, theatre or cinema tickets or courses to learn a new skill

- **Appreciate the benefits**
  Don't take the benefits of decluttering for granted. Take time to notice the space, light or order that you've created. Take pleasure in locating your keys within moments or packing for your holiday with ease. It's important to praise others for their part but don't forget to pat yourself on the back too

Whether you share your home with others or live alone, clutter can be an ongoing challenge but taking pre-emptive action will help you and your family to keep it at bay. Don't worry if your home doesn't look perfect; just set realistic goals, take pride in your efforts and enjoy the results.

Some Final Thoughts

Clutter is surreptitious. It accumulates gradually and imperceptibly but when it reaches a critical level it becomes impossible to ignore. Some of my clients liken it to an ever-present background noise, like piped music, mildly distracting but tolerable. But when the volume reaches a certain level it starts to interfere with your ability to hear or think straight.

You don't have to do it all on your own

If clutter in your home is getting in your way, literally or metaphorically, I hope this book has helped to start shifting your mindset and that you now feel able to take some action.

Getting started is often the hardest part so congratulate yourself for taking those first vital steps. Be bold. Be brave. Stay positive but pace yourself and take plenty of breaks. Decluttering can be exhausting, both physically and emotionally, so take time after each session to process your thoughts and rest your body and mind.

Remember that you don't have to do it all on your own – there's no shame in asking for help. Enlist a willing friend, relative or neighbour to keep you company while you declutter, or maybe ask someone you trust to become an accountability partner. Tell them what you intend to do and when you will do it. Then report back and share your success. By making yourself accountable, you're more likely to achieve your goals.

It's easy to underplay success so watch out for what I call 'tip of the iceberg' syndrome: bemoaning the work outstanding rather than celebrating achievements. Every full bin bag or delivery to the recycling centre or charity shop is a victory.

Although decluttering feels like a modern antidote to current materialist tendencies, it's by no means a recent concept. Thousands of years ago philosopher Rabbi Hillel said, 'The more possessions, the more worries'.[38] His words are as relevant now as they were then. Clutter weighs you down, saps your energy and takes up valuable physical and emotional space. So take a deep breath and overcome those excuses. When you take control of your environment and your clutter you'll be taking control of your life and making space for positive change and valuable experiences, projects and relationships. You'll find decluttering is a truly liberating experience with far-reaching effects so let your stuff go and make room for more happiness.

---

38   *Hillel, Ethics of the Fathers, 2:8*

Acknowledgements

Taking the leap from academic teaching to professional organising was the best career decision I ever took. But I wouldn't have been brave enough to do it without the guidance and support of my family and close friends. Most of all I'd like to thank my parents Mark and Naomi Pope, my brother and sister-in-law, Jon and Helen Pope, and my wonderful children Amitai and Elisheva.

I'd also like to express appreciation to my professional community, APDO Association of Professional Declutterers & Organisers, especially fellow members of our training team: Ingrid Jansen, Lesley Spellman, Sarah Bickers, Jasmine Sleigh and our dear friend Clare Parrack. Thanks to Cassie Tillett, who founded APDO in 2004 and put the UK organising industry on the map, and to all the volunteers, past and present, who serve on APDO's board. Our conversations constantly inform and inspire me.

Many friends have also shared wisdom and encouragement. Thanks in particular to Sheila Aarons, Sabha Arbabha, Rivka Caroline, Sally Cartwright, Ronit Knoble, Marcia Plumb, Nicole Robinson, Miriam Shire and Carolyn Spinks.

Much gratitude to Joanne Henson for conceptualising and editing the What's Your Excuse? series with such panache, and to Annette Peppis for such stylish designs.

Finally I'd like to thank all the clients who open their homes and their hearts, exploring issues relating to clutter, the universe and everything. I learn from you every day.

About the Author

Juliet Landau-Pope MA (Oxon), PGCertAP, CPCC, FHEA is a certified coach, professional organiser and study skills expert in London. An Oxford graduate, she has more than twenty-five years' experience of working in adult education as a university lecturer, researcher, editor, mentor, coach and consultant.

In 2008 she founded JLP Coach to provide a portfolio of services including practical decluttering and study skills coaching for adults and teenagers. She also leads innovative training in community and corporate settings to improve organisation and time management and volunteers as a board member (head of training) for APDO Association of Professional Declutterers & Organisers.

She features regularly in the media and has also written "What's Your Excuse for not Being More Productive?"

Find out more at:
www.jlpcoach.com
Email: juliet@jlpcoach.com
Facebook: www.facebook.com/declutter
Twitter: @jlpcoach
Instagram: @jlpcoach

Index

Also in this series

What's Your Excuse for not Being More Productive?

Juliet Landau-Pope
Overcome your excuses, stop procrastinating, get things done

Do you struggle to organise your time? Do you spend too much time planning and not enough time doing? Or are you simply unable to get started with things? Then this is the book for you.

Professional organiser Juliet-Landau Pope takes a look at all of the things you might be telling yourself to explain why you're not being as productive as you'd like, and offers practical advice, ideas and inspiration to help you move forward.

Don't know where to start? Don't have the time? Or do you simply feel overwhelmed? This supportive and motivational book will help you to tackle all of those beliefs and many more so that you can use your time more effectively in order to *get things done*.

Paperback – ISBN 978-0-9956052-2-0
e-book – ISBN 978-0-9956052-3-7

Also in this series

What's Your Excuse for not Overcoming Stress?

Kelly Swingler
Overcome your excuses for less stress and more control, calm and resilience

Do you struggle with stress in your life? Do you feel out of control, overwhelmed, under pressure or unable to relax?

In this supportive and motivational book Kelly Swingler takes a look at all of the reasons why you may be tolerating stress in your life. She explains how you can take action to reduce it and offers practical strategies, simple tips, guidance and inspiration to help you bring about positive change.

Learn how to switch off from the things you can't change and take control of those you can, to feel calmer, happier and more positive about yourself and your life.

Paperback – ISBN 978-0-9933388-6-8
e-book – ISBN 978-0-9933388-7-5

Also in this series

What's Your Excuse for not Eating Healthily?

Joanne Henson
Overcome your excuses and eat well to look good and feel great

Do you wish you could eat more healthily and improve the way you look and feel, but find that all too often life gets in the way? Do you regularly embark on healthy eating plans or diets but find that you just can't stick with them? Then this is the book for you.

This isn't another diet book. Instead it's a look at the things which have tripped you up in the past and offers advice, ideas and inspiration to help you overcome those things this time around.

No willpower? Hate healthy food? Got no time to cook? Crave sugary snacks? Overcome all of these excuses and many more. Change your eating habits and relationship with food *for good*.

Paperback – ISBN 978-0-9933388-2-3
e-book – ISBN 978-0-9933388-3-0

Also in this series

What's Your Excuse for not Being Better With Money?

Jo Thresher
Overcome your excuses and get to grips with your personal finances

Do you wish you could be savvier with money but find it too daunting? Do you wish you were more in control of your finances but find yourself avoiding taking action? Then this is the book for you.

Personal finance expert Jo Thresher takes a look at all of the reasons you might give for not getting to grips with your money, and offers advice, ideas and inspiration to help you change that.

No time to get organised? Scared to look at your bank statement? Think you're a shopaholic? Not money minded? Overcome all of these excuses and many more. Improve your relationship with your cash and feel more secure, more relaxed and more in control.

Paperback – ISBN 978-0-9956052-0-6
e-book – ISBN 978-0-9956052-1-3

Also in this series

What's Your Excuse for not Living a Life You Love?

Monica Castenetto
Overcome your excuses and lead a happier, more fulfilling life

Are you stuck in a life you don't love? Have you reached a point where your life doesn't feel right for you anymore? Then this book is for you.

This is not yet another self-help book claiming to reveal the secret to permanent happiness. Instead, it helps you to tackle the things which have been holding you back and gives ideas, advice and inspiration to help you move on to a better life.

Don't know what you want? Scared of failure? Hate change? Worried about what others might think? This book will help you overcome all of your excuses and give you the motivation you need to change your life.

Paperback – ISBN 978-0-9933388-4-7
e-book – ISBN 978-0-9933388-5-4

Also in this series

What's Your Excuse for not Loving Your Job?

Amanda Cullen
Overcome your excuses and change the way you feel about your work

Do you have a job which you're not enjoying as much as you know you should? Do you dread Mondays, spend your free time worrying about your work or feel undervalued by your boss or colleagues? If so, this book is for you.

In this supportive and motivational book Amanda Cullen takes a look at the wide variety of excuses we use which keep us stuck and unhappy in our work. She offers ideas and advice on how to tackle issues so that you can take control, make the necessary changes and transform your working life.

Don't like your colleagues? Spend too long in the office? Not confident in your skills? Or just plain bored? Overcome all of these and many more, and learn how to love your job.

Paperback – ISBN 978-0-9933388-6-1
e-book – ISBN 978-0-9933388-7-8

Also in this series

What's Your Excuse for not Getting Fit?

Joanne Henson
Overcome your excuses and get active, healthy and happy

Do you want to be fit, lean and healthy, but find that all too often life gets in the way? Do you own a gym membership you don't use, or take up running every January only to give up in February? Then this is the book for you.

This is not yet another get-fit-quick program. It's a look at the things which have prevented you in the past from becoming the fit, active person you've always wanted to be, and a source of advice, inspiration and ideas to help you overcome those things this time around. Change your habits and attitude to exercise for good.

Too tired? Lacking motivation? Bored by exercise? You won't be after reading this book!

Paperback – ISBN 978-0-9933388-0-9
e-book – ISBN 978-0-9933388-1-6

Also in this series

What's Your Excuse for not Being More Confident?

Charlotta Hughes
Overcome your excuses, increase your confidence, unleash your potential

Do you feel you could achieve much more in life if only you had more confidence? Do you know you'd be happier if you were braver, or had more self-belief? Then this is the book for you.

In this supportive and motivational book former Life Coach of the Year Charlotta Hughes takes a look at all of the ways in which we hold ourselves back and avoid expanding our horizons and she offers advice, ideas and inspiration to help change things.

Scared of failure? Feel unappreciated? Hate change? Worried about what others might think? This book will help you overcome all of your excuses and give you the motivation you need to change the way you feel about yourself.

Paperback – ISBN 978-0-9933388-8-5
e-book – ISBN 978-0-9933388-9-2

CN00661255

Icarus

and other poems

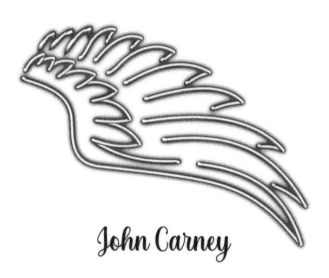

John Carney

Published by Key & Candle, Inc.
Jupiter, Florida

ISBN:
978-1-953666-13-0

eBook ISBN:
978-1-953666-14-7

John Carney is a novelist, poet, playwright, editor, and designer. His debut novel, Jupiter, was hailed as "a memorable literary achievement." He resides in Florida with his dogs, Mario and Luna.

τῇ καλλίστῃ

— *JC* —

Table of Contents

The Old Gods

To see my gods, I went to Rome,
And there I sat beneath the dome —
No more Jupiter and no more Mars,
My gods who rest among the stars.

I knelt before the Pantheon,
And there I couldn't help but weep
As I thought of all the secrets gone
The old gods used to keep.

Now all my gods have been replaced,
The victims of so many popes.
They, howe'er, will ne'er compare —
Despite their deepest, darkest hopes.

Helios' Son

Icarus wasn't the only one
To die from flying too close to the sun;
Hardly a mother's suffered worse despair
Than when Phaëthon took his father's chair.

He was merely a boy when he called on his sire,
The god of the chariot that brings the day's fire;
At e'ry daybreak, he drains dark from the night,
Helios Megistos, the bringer of light!

When Phaëthon arrived, his father was absent;
The boy waited unsurely, a solitary combatant.
Then came a sight from the end of the hall —
A brightness unfettered curved 'round the wall.

'Twas Sol's burning light of white luminescence
From a platinum diadem preceding his presence.
There the great god first confronted his issue;
After taking his measure, the meeting continued.

When he entered the room, Phaëthon's vision failed,
And when it returned, he found he had quailed.
With purple robes, on an emerald throne,
In a shining court, the light all his own —

So sat Helios Terpsimbrotos,
Who fathered the hero demanding his focus.

"Why come you to me?" asked the great, glowing god.
"I've come for what's mine," said his son with a nod.
"Don't ask me for this, you ignorant blight!"
"Don't deny me this thing that's mine by birthright!"

The god bit his tongue, pursuing a plot,
Then slowly he smiled at the thought that he caught.
Standing at once, he marched out of the palace,
His countenance showing neither pleasure nor malice.

With his scion in tow, shining Helios coursed:
To the left, Mons Olympus, to the right, a grand forest;
Over vast canyons, past great waterfalls;
Finally, he stopped before four marble stalls.

"I'll let you, my son, fly yearly on these,"
Acceded Helios Hesperionides.
"Once every year, my task will be yours,
And with it command of my fiery four:

Pyrois, the fiery one; and Aethon, the blazing;
Eous, who turns the sky; and Phlegon, the flaming.
You shall have what you seek; I'll not make you a duffer,
But if you find you're too meek, 'tis your fate to suffer."

John Carney

The god turned his back on the lad grown imperious,
The last Phaëthon saw of Helios Eleutherios.
Then the boy took the reins of those 'lympian steeds,
Ignoring scorched palms from their radiant leads.

He leapt into the cart, becoming eponymous,
Forsaking a life that was safe and anonymous.
Over blankets of dew and morning mist,
Those horses responded to every flick of his wrist.

He sent them on twists and tittles and tumbles —
A fanciful flight of frolics and gambols.
The steeds then grew bold and tilted toward high,
Rising higher yet higher into darkening sky.

The chariot lunged with a reel and a jerk,
And Phaëthon cursed his hands and their work.
Slipping toward Earth, felt his toes find the ledge
As he nearly fell out of his perfervid sledge!

Like a pip on the rim of a cup primed to spill —
Phaëthon clung, lurching higher yet still.
The Earth, far below, plunged deep into cold
As it stormed and it snowed and it froze at the poles.

Then, by some mercy, he caught hold of the reins,
Feeling like ichor flowed in his veins;
He knew in an instant his father's true power,
And his feelings of joy and exultance turned sour,

And just as his heart turned, so did his four;
They pointed their noses down toward the floor.
Together they dropped like a nugget of lead,
The boy's face whitening as the blood fled his head.

Down, down, the Earth, now caught in a blaze
As the chariot's rays countless cities did raze.
Whole swaths of land went up in flames,
Creating the deserts which then had no names.

And Phaëthon then, nearly frozen in fear,
Again lost the reins, dangling painfully near.
There hung the leads; they were just out of reach
From the tips of his fingers — an impenetrable breach.

He scoured his mind for some cheat or some trick,
His thoughts racing like gravity as he fell like a brick,
But his mind was too slow; he had already died
When a great flash of lightning rent through the sky,

And with it a blast like the end of the world hit —
Or was it a laugh from the one who had hurled it?

John Carney

Achilles

Ten years I've been at Troy,

But I don't trust time anymore.

All I have left is facade;

My uncle's walls taunt me

From across an ocean of sand.

Kronos twists the string of fate

Around his fingers, serpentine.

As the fingers twist, Atlas shifts,

And the world upon his back

First turns this way then turns back.

Ten years I've been at Troy,

But I don't trust time anymore.

Odysseus

Ten years I've been at sea,

But I don't trust my mind anymore.

All I have left is a dream of shore;

My mates have all died on me.

Something haunts me, something hunts me

Across an endless expanse of wine dark sea.

The wind tastes of some god's anger –

All ash and dirt and smoke and salt.

Father Trident strikes his trident

Against my prow, percussively.

Ten years I've been at sea,

But I don't trust my mind anymore.

John Carney

The Dogs of Ferlinghetti

I sailed to San Francisco on failing wings,
      Roamed the streets like a vagrant,
           Saw dogs sleeping in doorways.
They were huddled, hardened, hibernating things,
   and I was humbled.
They are still there. They live a separate life.
They fight secret wars in the parks over territory
   and decency standards.
They are bigger and smaller than me,
   both limited and free.

NIHIL OMNIA EST

Last night I was drifting in a spaceship.
> O capsule! My capsule!

Everything was white and there was room enough only
for one.

Screaming in terror, I floated through an endless sea of
emptiness.
> HIC MIHI CARMEN CANTARE

Every movement restricted, I wailed and I wept on my
solitary journey.

The night before last I was marooned on a wandering
comet.
> My home sweet home.

I watched existence itself dissolve before my
disbelieving eyes.

I saw distant stars and convenient planets transmogrify
and explode,
And I was enraptured by the awesomeness of nothing
and no one.

John Carney

The Call of Winter

The call of winter is a silent signal
To all in fall's twilight,
Not all who hear but all who listen
And read the lengthening night.

It rings like a bell that hasn't been rung,
A promise of something soon to come;
It plays like a melody from a song left unsung
But heard every night until winter is done.

The eve may be dark yet somehow still light —
A haloed moon in the haze, full and silver and bright —
Or no silver nor stars apparent through sight,
And a frosty wind blows, yet all still feels right.

To you who trust in what the call will bring —
Like peals of laughter from the bell it won't ring.
Or a soaring voice from the song it won't sing —
To you, winter gives all the joy 'neath her wing.

The call of winter is a silent signal
To all in fall's twilight.
Not all who hear but all who listen
And read the lengthening night.

And when the call's drowned by the showers of spring,
And when summer blazes ignite and engulf,
And when the days of fall die one by one,

Remember that winter's as wise as it's old,
So be silent and listen for the quiet and cold.

John Carney

"I fucking hate this town!"

I heard the man on the television —
From across an ocean and another of time —
And he spoke my words.

I hate this town.

I hate the private jet sales people,
Their painted faces slathered across benches and
billboards and bumpers and broadsides
Inside my fucking head.

I hate the country clubs, I hate the yachts,
I hate all the things your parents bought —
Or stole.

I hate the vultures in Italian cars,
And the made up lizards in upscale bars;
I hate the snakes that slither around
Among the carcasses that litter the ground.

The Nature of Everything

Esprit de Corpse

I've read the poems —
I still won't go
Won't fight
Won't buy
Whatever yarn
They're spinning this time.

For ours is to question why
Before we put our lives on the line —
That thin red line separating peace from war
Like the mark the Hebrews put above their doors.

A Dirge for the Fallen

Do you remember when we went to war?
　　When the hand of Death knocked at our door?

Together we huddled and laughed at Death,
　　But today we pause to catch our breath.

Our time of strength has not yet passed,
　　Although it seems beyond our grasp.

For together we lived, and together we fought,
And together we'll mourn what Fate has wrought.

John Carney

A Hope for the Future

To you, the denizens of that sparkling jewel of the mind, the future:

My sincerest hope for you is that your existence be blissfully free from the frustration of traversing the interstate highway alongside that ungainliest of all behemoths, that most unnatural of all beings, that numerically-modified noun — the eighteen-wheeler.

In fact, I hope you know nothing about this creature that is colloquially called the truck-trailer or trailer-truck; the semi-trailer and its truncated cousin, the semi; and, the apex of all the eighteen-wheeler's monikers, the Big Rig.

To travel near one of these beasts — whether ahead or behind, abreast or aside — is to experience a frustration unlike any other; it is a cold frustration, like a flickering fingerling of blue flame frozen in place, and oh how it burns. They crouch and they cruise, objects in the mirror more monstrous than they appear; they creep and they crowd, rumbling nearer and nearer; they crank and they crawl, crisscrossing the country, ever in thrall to the steerer's fear of being crushed in a crash and croaking like that and abruptly becoming an object of sundry and vulgar attention worth neither apprehension nor mention by those who crane their necks to satisfy their incomprehension, perplexed by the source of their untimely detention.

I hope instead that your shipping needs are accomplished by some mechanism that is fuel efficient and ethically fueled, carbon neutral and naturally cooled, responsibly sourced, vegan friendly, self-enforced, of course, and delivers you plenty for a fraction of a penny.

But I do hope so that you do not know how slow the Big Rig can go. They trundle along all wrong — first of all, they're much too long and everywhere always huddled in throngs. They clog up the roads, bogged down with their loads; they hog every lane, dogged by the specter of trains and planes and little hovering drones controlled by smartphones, hundreds of minuscule clones all independently owned and flying in newly apportioned zones.

And I hope that you have the opportunity to despise each of these things and wish for the days when shipping was restricted to the ground where the Big Rigs were found, and things only went where the Big Rigs were bound.

John Carney

Poems about Cars

Muir and Thoreau got to write about trees.
No poetry about cars from them.
Christina Rossetti wrote about love.
Not a word from her about running out of gas.
Lau-Tzu never fixed a flat all along his wavy Way,
And Rumi never learned how to hook up jumper cables.
I wonder if Whitman would have changed his own oil
Or if a thousand griots across a hundred generations
    would have told poems to one another about the
    technology behind variable valve timing.

Highway Privacy

A man in a Mercedes smokes a fat cigar.
He doesn't see me beside him in my car.
But, then again, what does he see?
Surrounded by mirrors yet blind as can be —
This must be highway privacy,
Where everyone can see you but you haven't a care;
Change lanes, no signal, a crash way back there,
But consequences aren't for him, no, poor dear;
They're the brunt that the rest of us suffer to bear,
And we can all of us see what's happening here,
But he's got his cigar, fancy car, and a buzz from the bar.

John Carney

A Winter Poem

It is night, dark and cold,
And I sit watching the snow fall outside my window.
The lamppost stands a silent sentry,
>Its beefeater hat growing by the hour atop a
>>glowing but vacant visage;

The boughs dip low of all the trees,
>More laden with snow than leaves;

Icicles slowly inch their way into existence,
>Ever so slowly.

I watch my footprints fill and disappear.
A faint trough is left behind but it too will soon be gone.
I want to go out and listen; I want to hear the sound of
>snow falling —
>>Soft static calling out within a vacuum tube.

But my dog is asleep beside me and he has earned his
>warm repose.

Instead, I look outside my window at the night
>swallowed by the storm,
>>The storm swallowed by the night.

Is the whole world not white beyond my window?

H _ N G M _ N

Have you heard of the man who lost all his hope?

I hear he's quite nearly at the end of his rope.

Not nearly.

How not?

Because he's quite reached the knot.

John Carney

<u>XVII</u>

"Seventeen times."

The man squirmed in his chair. He wished he hadn't've asked the question. Wondered for a moment about contractions before his mind continued along its circuitous path. He wished he had better clothes for the occasion too. As covertly as possible, he looked down at his pants. Why, God? Why, oh why, had he chosen pinstripes? Pinstripes hadn't been fashionable for years, but it was his best suit — his only suit these days.

He didn't like the chair they had offered him either, didn't feel it was befitting a man of his station — not that he knew what that was these days — and never mind how far his stock had fallen recently, so to speak. The chair was stiff; it had no give. Although made of wood, it felt like metal — lifeless. He scraped his fingernails against the grain, wondered how many other men had sat there, remembered his question. He frowned.

They were cut short — his fingernails that is. Didn't think it'd make a difference, but, hey, who knew these days? He knew he shouldn't let his mind wander, but it had gotten so hard to focus lately. The doctor had said something about it — given it a fancy name — but he had never been one for remembering fancy names even before the diagnosis. No need for the State to know about this, she had said with a wink. Didn't like the State much, his doctor; he remembered that much. Kept going on about how they get in the way of all manner of business. He didn't know about all that, but he didn't interrupt; he liked her, his doctor. She had the same delicate, grey curls that his mother had had in her later years.

She had smelled cloyingly of gardenia flowers though — his mother, that is, not his doctor. Not always, you understand, just the last time he saw her. In fact, it was the church that had smelled of gardenia, but he didn't know that — never would know it either. All he knew was that he smelled gardenia whenever he thought of his mother lately.

He had the sense of waiting on a phone call, but he couldn't remember why. Something important, it seemed, but then, how important could it've been if he'd forgotten it?

"Yep, pulled this'yer switch seventeen times before."

He wanted to nod — show he understood the significance of the other man's statement — but a strap of leather, about two inches thick, ran across his forehead.

It smelled new, he thought, not much at all like gardenia.

ISO : world class poetry

Requirements:
>Exactly thirty-five lines.
>Lines must not rhyme!
>Poems must discuss things that are deep,
>>like death but not so dark;
>Must pursue profound themes with a paucity of
>>remarks;
>Must be poetic but not overly so;
>Must be ascetic with an orator's flow;
>Must be ironic but not insincere;
>Must not ruin a polite atmosphere;
>Must incorporate style without any pedantry;
>Must be repetitive, treating words as a tenantry;
>Must be willing to work for no pay;
>Must receive submissions by yesterday!

In short:
>Not too bland, not too grand, not too avant-
>garde,
>But poems must not be too hard to understand.

>(Bear in mind: LINES MUST NOT RHYME!)

States of Matter(ing)

Are you liquid?

I thought about it, said no.
Thought about it some more, decided I was.
  At least seventy percent according to Science.

So I said so.

Not what the mortgage man meant,
  His trained eye focused on some line or other of
    figures.

I'm more liquid than solid or gas,
  But

None of that seems to matter.

John Carney

Luckies

We eat our mushrooms in the car — mix them with chocolate, peanut butter, orange juice… anything to mask the flavor really; that and the knowledge that at least a smear of cow shit probably lingers somewhere among the spongy contents of the clear plastic bag.

"The vitamin C helps," says a pink-haired pixie with a pierced eyebrow.

I masticate my own handful of caps and stems as furtively as possible, the tang of the orange juice nearly masking the must and dirt. I gag, manage to swallow a stringy stem with the help of another gulp of golden fire. It feels magical in my mouth, this $1.95 orange juice from 7-11. The pixie said it helps. I eat my final two caps — each the size of a nickel — in a spoonful of peanut butter.

Four cigarettes blaze like censers as we make our way down the beach. Silver-tipped waves wash the moonlight over the water. Mercurial dew drops already dot the wooden chairs. They belong to the resort, but the time of hotels laying claim to the beach has long since ended for the day, their residents safely pickled in martinis since the sun went down. Now, the beach belongs to us.

Clouds move swiftly across the sky, a regatta of ungainly apparati. They follow the rules of the sky, each falling in line with the flow of the rest. They watch us on the beach. To them, we are silver-tipped and mercurial too, four moon-soaked wanderers.

The clouds aren't alone in their flight. Palm trees bend in the wind, their capitals yearning to break free from their moorings and take to the sky.

Happiness is a color and the color is me.

We leave when the buildings start to sway like palm trees in the breeze.

A spaceship hurtling through inky darkness.

John Carney

Lucky's

We sat on a low, concrete curb, James and I. The air carried the sound of rushing water or maybe the wind — undeniably an ocean sound, whatever it was. We smoked in silence, our two cigarette tips burning like fireflies in the night, flaring up momentarily before floating haphazardly in trails of fading light. I picked at the curb's coarse surface.

James' face was blue. Not the mottled blue of a goblin nor the cold blue of a demon, but a calm blue — placid, pacific. I didn't tell him his face was blue, assumed it was the mushrooms we had eaten on the beach — James, Joe, Ashley, and I. We had dragged wooden lounge chairs together, their feet leaving deep grooves in the sand, and sat in the salt breeze from the sea, palm trees swaying, clouds blowing across the sky like milk foam. We left when the buildings began to sway with the trees; piled into James' car, and drove, drove, drove — a ship sailing on the sea of the night. The lines in the road raced past us like shooting stars. I closed my eyes, but the stars continued rushing toward me, through me. When I opened them again, the lines had stopped moving. So had the car.

A large, ovoid sign glowed overhead.

Lucky's, it said, humming softly.

But that had been minutes ago… years really.

Joe and Ashley were gone now, somewhere far away it seemed although I couldn't remember, not really.

My firefly burned out, died. I pulled a disposable plastic lighter from my pocket, clicked it once-twice-thrice until a flame sprang from the tip, brought my firefly back to life. We smoked in silence, James and I, skeins of smoke drifting through cones of pale yellow light.

A loud, clangorous bell shattered the night, cracks spreading across the darkness like strands of spider silk. Joe and Ashley fell out of an open doorway — two drops of honey dripping out of a jar, hesitant at first and then giddy in their acceleration.

James stood up, pitched his cigarette butt into the black. He pulled the lever on the gas nozzle sticking out of the side of his car and the rushing noise stopped. The air was still, quiet. Joe and Ashley melted against the side of the car, managed to operate the door handle, tumbled inside.

I stood, sent the corpse of my firefly after its friend, cast a diffident look across the roof of the car at James.

Better places to smoke, eh?

We grinned at one another, then got in the car and sailed back into the darkness.

John Carney

The House at the Top of the World

In a city upon a hill
Where light is long and air is thin
There is a house to take you in —
The house at the top of the world.
   Fear not!
  The house is quite old
  And haunted, of course,
  By the corpses of works
  That died 'fore their births
  And the ghosts of those
  Who wrote by the hearth
  And left us such books
  Of considerable worth.
And in that city upon that hill
Is a place worth making a pilgrimage —
  A place to take a wandering in,
For what might you find in that paramount mine
Full of lies made of truths and truths made of lies?
Home of fictions and fables of every kind
And myths and legends from many a mind.
But the house is a place which doesn't exist,
  Or, at least, it doesn't in the way that it is;
In the here and the now, 'tis a mere residence,
  But will soon, perhaps, fulfill its promise.

Forty Cents

Mountains and molehills, mountains and molehills.

What's forty cents, after all?

A fountain made of spilled milk bowls.

I'll die on a forty-cent hill

Because money is relative and so are mountains.

He was an alchemist.
The way he took that powder,
Loose as sugar,
And turned it into liquid,
Heating it at the end of a spoon,
Its head discolored from the flames of
A thousand disposable Bic lighters.
In a moment, he had filled a syringe
With his concoction,
The plunger pulled back and ready —
Ready to deliver that
Unbelievable
Incontestable
Unstoppable
Rush of warmth and joy
As it travels down, down my bloodstream.
Echoing waves of endorphins
Crash upon the beachhead of pain.
Nerves sizzle in white hot fire
As muscles stretch and strain
And try to remain
Tense
And
Taut
And
Tight
And
Caught…
Caught fire in the reverie and
Caught in the fire of reverie.

Last Man's Dais

I met an old man from a foreign land,
Who knelt — blind and naked — on golden sand.
Blood from his knees had ere stained the ground;
He'd been there so long the red had gone brown.
He wore, like a fig leaf, two cupped palms,
Not there for shame but for gathering alms.
His face bore contentment, a lack of concern,
Free from any emotion that I could discern.
He moved not a muscle when I came near,
And yet I could tell — he knew I was there.
Suddenly he moved — too quick to be seen —
One hand disappeared from where it had been.
He had raised that hand and shielded his eyes,
And without a sight, saw my every disguise.
  Lo! Two black marks on the back of his hand.
    One was a key to unlock any door,
    The other a candle, burning no more.
    No hole for the key and nary a flame
    On the hand of the man who hadn't a name.
  Hark! What came next, what left me unmanned.
He sat quite still as he darkened the skies
And silenced the sound of my forthcoming cries.
He reached out with fingers, so brittle and mean,
Then curled all but one, especially lean,

And pierced my soul with the tip of that spear.
"Do not be afraid — you've nothing to fear.
One day to death — to me — you'll return,
But never to suffer and never to burn.
Although you've not heard them, I've my own psalms,
And salves and saviours and magical balms.
I AM THE FALLEN," he said without sound,
And at last I discovered what I had found.
Then he put the black marks upon my own hand
With an ancient needle he pulled from the sand.

John Carney

Florida

Thing about Florida is, it's hot.
    "It's the humidity that'll getcha."
    That's what everybody says. All of them.
    And they're right — obviously — but they're still
        annoying.

The night is full of noise.
    A bird croaks. Again. Again.
    The wind rustles the palm trees, their fronds the
        accordion folds of a hand fan.
    A frog croaks. Again. Again.
    The chirping of a million and one incessant insects
        fades into the aether.
    An alligator croaks. Again. Again.
    Bird. Frog. Alligator. Bird. Frog. Alligator.
    They've been at this a while.

Some nights are hot.
    The air hums with the tickle of electricity, and sweat
        prickles across exposed skin.
Some nights are cool, though.
    Especially when clouds whisper a tale about winter,
        A tale told from afar, voyeuristically.

It's not too hot for the birds and the frogs and the
    alligators. Not yet.

<u>*Politically Adept*</u>

A white bird alights on the shore of a pond.

An alligator — too orange to blend into either the myriad greens or dull greys that reflect off of the water's surface around his craggy skull — skulks in the shallows. He doesn't like the depths beyond, preferring it here where the fruit hangs low.

The white bird wades. The gamboge alligator waits.

It happens in a moment — a flash, a splash, and the white bird's neck is snapped.

Now what rough beast, its hour come round at last, Slouches towards the swamp to sojourn?

John Carney

The Warmth

I'll tell you a secret:
The *snick* of the needle starts to feel good
As it slips into you through a hole in your skin.
The warm blanket is coming,
And the pain has been cold, so cold.

The needle presses down and the record starts to play.
Time dilates and fashions itself into a lento rhythm,
Riding on a length of red and violet ribbon.
The warmth rushes through my veins like a flash flood
caught in slow motion.
I stand on a bank that threatens to wash away, filming
myself in that flood,
But there's a fire inside my flotsam corse.
I'm past, looking back at myself as the water flows around
me.
I'm standing on the promontory, the merciful water
surrounds me.

My present is warm and clean and free.

"My Fingers Hurt"

The world was black around him; he was enshrouded by darkness itself, the memory of his eyes sharp and bitter. He struggled against the pit — clawing at the muddy walls, stripping more flesh from his bloody fingertips with every handful of moist dirt. He pawed at root and rock and raw earth — through the pain of despair and lost fingernails, snapped off in the mad scrabble. His blood shone atop and among the mud — its crimson brightness streaking the burnt sienna dirt. The bloody stripes shined in the moonlight of a humid jungle night.

John Carney

Everything Dies

Everything dies —
Persons, peoples, and even species.
One day, the last human will fall.
Black holes will eat stars whole.
Even galaxies will expire.
Finally, the vacuum of the universe
Will unplug and the motor
Will whir to a halt.
And what then?
Will an imploding universe explode
Out of the asshole of an atom?

Strophe and Antistrophe

The Universe ejaculates itself into existence.
Through the maelstrom of scientific chaos,
stars are born.
They expand,
contract,
combine,
collide,
and even die.
There are those that make our own sun look meek
And others that make it disappear entirely.

Perhaps one day a star will grow so large
That its death creates a black hole so strong
That it eats the entire Universe,
And shits out a new Big Bang.

John Carney

Small Talk

Are you afflicted?

Oh, yes. I have a condition.

Is it bad?

Terminal.

What's it called?

Existence.

Cigarette

The gentle crinkle of a hand-rolled cigarette,
  Full of green leaves
  Torn apart and sprinkled
  Along a paper eave.

That delicate cylinder clutched between fingertips,
  Smoke leaking from out of its orifice
  And staining nails browns and oranges.

The tip of my cigarette is a yellow star
  Interrupting constellations.

It dances though the sky,
  A firefly,
  A microscopic supernova tracing arcs and
  parabolae,
  A meteor with a wand'ring path,
  A planet's course devoid of math.

The fire fades, its light extinguished —
  Its life brief and undistinguished.

John Carney

A Name for a Dragon

A golden koi swims against the flow;
The water rushes past as steady as time;
Far off, somewhere, a font releases riparian rapids.

Scales as bright as newly minted coins,
And a whiskered face unmarked by woe;
Fins ache to be fingers with pointed claws.

The koi questions not the path;
It knows neither terminus nor failure;
Dragons have no need for names.

The Phoenix of Void And All Creation

Reborn from ash and smoke and cinders,
    Arise, Phoenix, arise.
Wake the world with your fiery call,
    Arise, Phoenix, arise.
The secrets of all creation are hidden in the colors
of your tail, written against the maw of the all
swallowing void.

John Carney

Pretend

"Be careful what you pretend to be."

Kurt Vonnegut wrote that, and it remains one of my favorite quotes. There's even a second part to it:

"Because you are what you pretend to be."

How hopeful. How terrifying.

I began pretending to be a writer many years ago — it is my favorite thing to pretend to be. Before that, I pretended to be a teacher; before that, a soldier. I still enjoy pretending to teach sometimes, but I never much cared for pretending to help kill people. I just wanted to pretend to run obstacle courses, really.

Oh boy! What power there is in pretend!

Vonnegut was a soldier too — and a teacher.

Oops. I mean he pretended to be. Now he's pretending to be dead. Doing a damn fine job of it too. Almost as damn fine a job as he did of pretending to be a writer.

Anyway. What are you pretending to be?

For most of my life, I have lived in the woods.

Ok, wait. Let's get that straight.

I'm not saying I've lived like John Muir, swinging from a treetop in a gale or anything. Maybe more like Thoreau, making the short walk into town from Walden Pond and enjoying the abundance of nature.

You know, the rows of beans and direction of dreams and all that.

Except what we have in abundance in my neck of the woods are dead rabbits.

I fish them out of the pool;

I pry them from my dogs' mouths;

I shovel their corpses off of my yard;

and, when I make my own journey into town,

I dodge their smashed and shattered forms in the road.

Dead.

Done.

Undignified.

I know that soon I will be.

Just.

Like.

Them.

You will be too. Nothing against you: we all will be.

As for me, that is why I write — because I will soon be gone.

And just like those rabbits, I intend to leave a mark — Even if it's just a bloody splash in the street.

A Song of Spring

Spring!
    Spring!
A song of spring
And all the bounty a new season brings.
The snow is amelt and feeding the streams
With water that's cool and fast and clean.
And the sun is high in the bluebird sky,
Girded by clouds that trick the eye.

Spring!
    Spring!
A honeybee's sting
And the first gust of air 'neath a cardinal's wing.
New life abounds, touring the grounds,
Or takes to the air and heads out of bounds.
And the sun is high in the bluebird sky
Bathing the birds as they fly, rising high.

Spring!
    Spring!
Sealed with a ring,
A match made in heaven and fit for a king.
All things, large and small, seek out their thrall,
And return to the earth to crawl and to sprawl.
And the sun is high in the bluebird sky
Without any lies or thoughts of alibis

Spring!
    Spring!
My heart on a string
As I turn to things worth worshipping.
The sun and the sky, and the tides of fate,
The birds and the bees, and me and my mate.
And the sun is high in the bluebird sky
And it'll continue to rise long after I die.

John Carney

Coffeeshop Concerto

Blast of steam and a high-pitched whistle;
Pound pound, percussion on the countertop;
Hardened beans chip and fleck between the teeth
Of minuscule gears as they grind away in bursts.
A barista's voice motors a mile a minute
About milk types, merchandise, and mortgage rates.
Glaciers of milk foam collapse into an ocean of cold
coffee
Under the watchful eye of a bedraggled face
Reflected in gleaming copper and chrome.

Coffeeshop Sunrise

She bears the coffee cup like a Grail,
Passed with reverence across the concrete countertop.
When she meets my tired eyes,
I see the rising sun budding on horizons to the east —
Caught on that line between darkness and revelation;
Full of hope and raw beauty, the energy of life, and the
pure opportunity of a brand new day.
Across a countertop of concrete or a chasm of time and
space,
I bathe in the light and soak its warmth into my skin
gratefully.

John Carney

Loko

The sun is up.
The day's begun.
There's coffee in my cup,
And work to be done.

Milano

Diesel jeans and a black leather jacket,
Motorcycle boots with laces wrapped around the ankles,
A slim, sleek purse clutched in one hand,
Occhiali da sole from Liberace's closet,
Black hair, grey skies, and light-white foam atop a cup of
cappuccino —
Ehi, Milano, che fa oggi?

John Carney

Las Vegas

Two buildings cast from gold;
an obelisk, sphinx, and pyramid;
a Statue of Liberty in a castle's backyard,
a children's playset in the shadow of
a hulking casino-hotel-roller coaster combo;
and a golden lion with a mane of fire.

New York New York!
M&Ms, fast food, Coca-Cola, giant guitar;
there goes the world's oldest self-driving car;
Prada, Gucci, Louis Vuitton,
Waldorf Astoria, Dolce & Gabbana;
an enormous balloon, an Arc de Triomphe,
an Eiffel Tower that could fit in your palm;
Neptune's fountain, palace, and theater,
a palm tree garden and a campanile,
a Rialto Bridge without any water,
and two truncated executioner's columns.

Circus Circus! Circus Circus!
Twelve million lights in a billion-dollar circuit;
and Scarlet O'Hara in front of the Sahara,
and a squad of acrobats outside of the Strat,
and a saucer-shaped space ship sitting on a spindle.

Palm Beach

Welcome to Palm Beach!
Home to pedophiles, Ponzi schemers, and pilferers of
every stripe.
But that's not all!
We've got
a U.S. Attorney cutting sweetheart deals
for billionaires with highlight reels
of all the little boys and girls
and their partners from his Rolodex wheel;
we've got
Rockefeller inheritors and Vanderbilt heirs,
Presidential ejecta and then that of theirs,
a million market manipulators
with mansions made to match each other's;
we've got
drug-dealing chiefs of police with entire platoons of
pushers
and plenty of pretty little idiots just waiting to be
famous
-ly
used
and abused
and then tossed
like refuse.

Trash.
Garbage.
Thrown into the sea like a stripped and skeletal
carcass...

...and all was just aces until...Epstein was suicided inside of his cell.

John Carney

Legacy

The President's legacy is a line on a map;
The General's, a salute with a snap.
The Colonel's legacy is battles won,
But the soldier's legacy is merely a question,
A simple question:
"What have I done?"

Ants

Ant legs move like tiny clocks,
Ticking twigs that time they mark,
Marching sticks which never halt
While all around them all else doth.

Ants, they are like living death.
Without lungs they breathe no breath,
While they hoist their Atlantean hefts;
They've neither pride nor shibboleths.

Behold! The Lilliputian Myrmidons!
Fighting their puny Olympian skirmishes.
They are mighty, and they are minuscule,
And they the Earth with black bejewel.

John Carney

<u>Hymenogastraceae Psilocybe Cubensis; or,</u>
<u>The Talking Frog</u>

"Ribbit MOTHERFUCKER,"
The frog said in my head.

What he really said,
"Excuse me, my dear fell-
Ow, you look a tad unwell."

"Was that supposed to be a pun?"
I called into the night.

The War of Art

Art is a force multiplier.
It takes an idea and amplifies it, magnifies it, transports it.
Ideas expressed in art can outwit their critics, outspeak
    their competitors, and outlive their creators.
For how long can
    a song echo in your ear,
    a painting imprint on your eyes,
    and a story set a fire inside your heart?

John Carney

Growing Old

My asshole used to work like the irising lens of a fucking
   Nikon,
Like a rustic knife slicing a log of potato meal into
   gnocchi —
>   Plop, plop, plop,
>   They go as they drop;
>   Sploosh, splish, splash,
>   They fall out of my… pot.
But back to my asshole,
Once upon a time, it worked a charm like a mariner's
   arm;
But now the latch in my ass is more like a submarine's
   hatch,
Swinging open on rusty hinges and slamming shut with a
   clash.
And it isn't just my rectum that doesn't do what I
   expect'a'him —
There's my back and my knees, my shoulders and feet,
And don't get me started on each of my teeth.
My dick dribbles piss on my toes just a bit,
When I stand at the toilet thinking I'm finished,
And the only ache I don't have is the one I soon will.
But that's just growing old, I suppose,
And even Nikons and knives break down in the end.

Icarus

Flying through a sun shower
On a plane with paper wings
And a tiny two-stroke engine
With hardly half a horsepower

What could go wrong today?

John Carney

Milton Keynes UK
Ingram Content Group UK Ltd.
UKHW020950221123
433051UK00020B/803

John Carney

If You Give Up

poems from a dead lover's diary

Published by Key & Candle, Inc.
Jupiter, Florida

ISBN:
978-1-953666-13-0

eBook ISBN:
978-1-953666-15-4

John Carney is a novelist, poet, playwright, editor, and designer. His debut novel, Jupiter, *was hailed as "a memorable literary achievement." He resides in Florida with his dogs, Mario and Luna.*

To all my dead lovers,
May your graves be strewn with flowers forever.

— JC —

Table of Contents

Porcelain

Come
Melt on my tongue
Like a sugar cube.
Run down the channels
On the sides of my mouth
And drip from my chin
Like cream off of porcelain.

Daydream

Having a daydream of holding your hand
While the radio plays our favorite bands.
Digging our toes into warm, golden sand
And watching the sun set on faraway lands.

I'd spend every day with you just that way
Until the light turns grey and we both fade
away.

<u>*Origami*</u>

I want to fold your body like a piece of origami.
    To hold you in my hands
    And finger your folds and creases.

John Carney

Amoraroma

The salt of the ocean, an explosion of flowers,
A pot full of honey, and grass in rain showers.

A chocolate croissant and a strong cappuccino
With a warm brioche full of almond granita.

Garlic and onions, hot olive oil,
Salted pasta water comes to a boil.

Pizza and beer hang in the air
   all along the *Via Capoprati*.
Meanwhile, elsewhere, *giallorossi* fanfare
     serenades the night in the city.

the voodoo of a lude photograph

allure stripped bare
    stripped to naked skin
a liar's simple lair
    of unconsummated sin

nude and nubile
    or verily virile
either desired
    neither evil nor vile

whether drawn all in pink or perhaps just a hint —
    a loose slip of fabric and a peek at goose prickles
    tumescence or tumidity and, of course, engorgement

O, facsimile, facsimile, wherefore art thou, facsimile?
    you, manufactured distraction,
    you, promise of future satisfaction,
        constructing reality after a fashion:
    with a hint of dark hair — appetizer of passion —
        and a devilish stare, those tools of attraction

climax free of denouement,
    a flick of the wrist and a joyless yawn.

John Carney

Thunderstorms and Ghosts

Every day I wander.
Every night I wonder:
Where am I going?
And I know it's showing.

Wandering through the desert,
Walking alone along the coast,
I've got a paddle,
But I can't find my boat.

Every day it thunders;
I hear a distant roaring.
I won't go under
Even if it starts pouring.

I'll ride a rising tide;
I'll fight against a ghost,
But my boat will stay afloat,
And I'll get the ghost by the throat.

<u>*Every Word*</u>

every word I wrote
is going up in smoke —
I'm burning them down
on my way out of town.

you forgot something
when you left.
you didn't take me with you —
you never do.

John Carney

Something colorful in the trash,
I stooped and scooped them when I passed.
A dozen roses.
Dying.
Dead.
They look just like the blood I bled.

In that bouquet I see your head,
And more than that I see your face
Before you left without a trace.

Now your apparition fades,
And ne'er an act of contrition made.

●●●●● *#566*

Some
Days
All
I
Want
Is
To
Hurt
You
As
Badly
As
You
Hurt
Me

Unforgivable

"You unforgivable, you don't talk to me of pacts. There are no binding oaths between men and lions, wolves and lambs can enjoy no meeting of the minds, they are all bent on hating each other to the death. So with you and I." (The Iliad, 22.260)

There's a very cold and dark place in the deep
recesses of my heart.
It's where my hatred burns.
It's where you will live, forever;
Where the great gods of antiquity connive at
your demise;
Where retributive justice brings vindication.
It's where 'forgiveness' is just another word for
deception.

And it's a place you have no right to be because,
Desolate though it is,
It remains a piece of my heart,
And I've only got the one.

Endymion's Escape

It's been months and weeks and days and hours

Since flames engulfed our verdant bower.

I thought sleep would be my solace,

But you even haunt my dreams.

We used to sleep as one, we three;

A sleep so deep it set me free.

Now I know nothing's as it seems,

And only me and the dog make 'us.'

The bower is gone except for ashes,

And there you stand with a box of matches.

John Carney

Mantra

Her name became a mantra in my mouth.
Such magic in that name.

Words

"I'm not good with words," she said,
    Before eviscerating me
    With a string of them
    As sharp as a samurai sword.

John Carney

The Dark

We're all afraid of the dark.

It is an archetypal fear
Of what we know is hiding there —
A drowning woman with mottled skin,
Or a horde of ravenous skeletons,
Carnivorous doctors in a secret cabal,
Or a shark with teeth that are ten feet tall.

But the real reason we're all afraid is
Because the only monsters in the void
Are the ones we bring there with us.

Black All the Way Down

I know you hate me now.

Write it down —
    Black ink on a black page.
    Trap it all in a black envelope.
    Address it 'to Hell' and drop it in a fire.

I'll see it when I get there.

Another half-finished poem

I am a collector of half-started lives and hypothetical
wives.
 Half a soldier, half a scholar,
 Half a husband, half a father.
  As much as any, I am one —
  Which is to say that I am none.
 Half a decade at war, half a decade at school,
 Half a decade spent with each of half a dozen
different women:
  Every time I was half of a whole
  Now I'm just half — a rock with no roll.
 Half a lepidopterist pinning dead things,
 With sterile fingers, stretching their wings,
 And posing them here in a case behind glass;
 Imposing false order on my mental morass.
  Here half a butterfly, there half a moth,
  Everywhere half conquests I've never forgot.
I am half an arsonist burning down half a home,
And half a poet writing half of a poem.

Today / Tomorrow

1.
Today was good,
But it will not last.
I wish it could,
But it's already past.
What comes tomorrow,
Who can say?
Perhaps today
Was my last day.

2.
Tomorrow is another day and after that another.
They won't all be bad; we won't always suffer,
So let's see what they hold together.

I'll stay for you; you stay for me,
And each of us will see.

John Carney

XVIII

My ship weighs anchor, sails away.
"Forever and ever," I hear her say.
The rising sun lights the bay.

If You Give Up

The ship sails straight without a list.
Before the breeze, a windblown kiss.
The morning sun consumes the mist.

XVIII

The merry wind begins to die,
And darkened clouds have all drawn nigh.
The noontime sun hangs in the sky.

XVIII

XVIII

The violent sea casts the ship off her mark.

The storm hath battered and beaten the ark.

The afternoon sun hides in the dark.

John Carney

Lost! Alas, because of the squall,
Lost at sea; no hope at all.
The evening sun has begun to fall.

XVIII

XVIII

"When comes the end?" I hear her inquire.

"F're'er and a day or until I expire."

The setting sun lights the seas on fire.

John Carney

A Life that Never Could Have Been

As much as I lie to myself about it, once I loved you.
My heart beat and burned for you, and I was left with a
    burnt and beaten heart.
And although that bruised and bloodied thing lay pinned
    on the floor, you did not break it.
With all your might and all your weight, you did not
    break it.
But the pieces of gore that clung to your heel are yours
    Now —
    Mementos of a life that never could have been;
    A portrait of a wife who couldn't help but sin.
From the floor, I watched you walk away,
then waited…
                …waited…
                        …waited…
…for the return of Halcyon days.

Now I've turned my thoughts from such empty refuge
Since your port in the storm disguised the deluge.

Fragments

when it's cold outside
I close my eyes
and try to erase
your smiling face
from inside my mind.

I want to bury my face in your hair,
in your curls;
get lost with you
in our make believe world.

but I sleep alone now.
I wake up alone too.
I'm going back to sleep.

If Only

If only! If only!
    The little mouse cried,
But he couldn't break free
    No matter how hard he tried.

Whether clutched in the talons
    Or caught by the eye,
If only! If only!
    Is the imbecile's cry.

Reflections

Sitting on my patio
Playing a solo on
A glass trumpet
Pointed toward the floor.
It is a song about
A pink-haired pixie with a pierced eyebrow,
An olive-skinned Aphrodite in an apricot gown,
A plain-faced belle as sweet as pumpkin pie,
And an alabaster babe with an apple in her eye.

I shuffle through old photographs like they're potential
portals to the past,
And what price wouldn't I pay to pass through their
plastic paper?

A mound of ashes piles up before me
As I stare into my future.
Thoughts of mortality float like smoke
And anxiety fills my heart with petrol.
The bitter elixir burns blacker and thicker
As it spurs me toward its own end
And mine as well.

John Carney

Exhaustion

Your words are empty —

　　Like your head,

　　Like your heart.

You said my name so many times that now I'm empty too.

Pronouns

I dream of you,
And know it's wrong,
But at least
I'm not dreaming
About her anymore.

Stranger's Kindness

I fall in love four times a day —
Morning noon and night,
Then once more when I'm asleep
And seeing with dreamsight.

Every time I look, in fact,
I find another's just gone past.
I wonder if I've made a pact
With a dark'ning stranger
      by a railroad track.

Did I to him my soul a-sell?
For eyes that never can be still?
What a bargain for that fellow —
But what'd I get from the Devil?

Wrong Book

"Let's be on the same page," she said,
    And in that moment,
    I learned I was a slow reader.

The words that came next were unnecessary —
    I already knew which page I was on.
    I just thought she was there too.

John Carney

I Feel So Much Like Giving Up

We're all alone on our rotting pebble,
Floating in a muddy puddle.
Tear drops falling pitter-patter.
No one hears them; no one matters.

<u>Post Modern Pop Art</u>

(Inspired by ***Expensive Taste,*** by **Becky Rosa**)

There it was.
Stuck to the wall.

A piece
      Of Post
            Modern
                  Pop Art
                        Like
Lichtenstein on LSD or Salvador on DMT.

Melt on,
Magenta molasses,
Thick and sticky
Down the hand,
Down two-tone fingers
Implying definition,
Defying that tongue's
Licking
      Licking
           Licking

And just what —
Or who —
Is up to melting next?

John Carney

Behold, the Harpy!

(Inspired by **Meghan,** by **Rick Lazes**)

Behold, the Harpy!

Her wings —
    Terrible and hideous and beautiful —
    Blue blades pointed toward the
    Land of the living
    From these Elysian plains.

Her chest —
    Red and downy and bosomed with
    Powerful —
    Oh, so powerful —
    Muscles.

Tremble,
    Oh, mortals,
    Before she who knows the
    Secrets of your hearts.

<u>NO 5 BLEU</u>

(Inspired by *Marilyn En Bleu*, by **Sylvestre Gauvrit**)

With all the liquid energy of water,
Crash, crash against the dreadful might of
Lines and angles and
Glass and metal and
Time and space and
Normal and
Expected and
Dull as all the reasons why.

You,
Sapphire wave of
Sapphic grace,
You, you,
You bear that dress against the wind and
Beat beat beat
Onward against
Normal and
Expected and
Dull as all the reasons why.

John Carney

In Fiamme

Come un prigioniero di Plato
Chi era finalmente liberato,
Cosí lui esce della grotta,
E vede é stato un'idiota,
Quindi ride a crepapelle
Quando lui vede le stelle.

El Dia de los Muertos

Mictecacihuatl
Nosotros adoramos
Su la difunta
Difunta Catrina

    Los Muertos
    Caminan con nosotros
    Los Muertos caminan
    El Dia de los, el Dia de los Muertos

Antes de honrar a
Sus santos honramos
A nuestra propria
Los padres de nuestros padres

    Los Muertos
    Caminan con nosotros
    Los Muertos caminan
    El Dia de los, el Dia de los Muertos

John Carney

So I Say Goodbye

From the ramparts of Troy,
She said her goodbye —
"Goodbye, my Astyanax, good boy."
Then, Neoptolemus took her by his side.
Past a stain on a stair —
Streaks of red turning brown
And strands of blonde hair —
He led her back down.

I'll not go there.
Not go to that place
Where Cleopatra, Dido, Helen, and Semiramis
Are made by men to mourn men —
Like Achilles, Tristan, and Paris.

Senza Titolo

Every day
To myself I say,
"Will I ever love again?"

My heart says, "No,"
My head says, "Yes,
If you give up on revenge."

<u>Cerulean Dream</u>

I dream a dream in cerulean
And everywhere I look
The scene's a screen, hiding what's unseen
Like snowfall in a book.

Blue and blue and blue and blue,
In every shade and every hue,
But one especially just between —
The bluest blue and slightly green —
It is a dream of cerulean.

The blue behind a clouded sky,
The iris of a viking's eye,
The sea beneath a colorless sun,
A gemstone button come undone.

Blue and blue and blue again,
The very length of light transcends,
But nevertheless the color remains
Always just and just the same
In the cerulean dream.

Morphine Dream

I stare out my window at the palms and the pines.
Palm fronds hang like baleen cast off from a whale
swimming in the wind
While pine needles disappear into the clouds.

I lay in my bed, unable to rise.
The world through my window is a wonderful thing.
The pain stays inside.
Clouds like dollops of frothed milk — if I brush my finger
through them, will I discover the same delicate, geometric,
structured bubbles?

The curtains are coming apart at the seams.
Threadbare and raw,
The weave wears itself against itself.

A pterodactyl talon tears tendons through my back
As a youth wasted on loose women flashes through my
mind.

John Carney

Baths

No job, no money, no food.
Body's broken — can't move.
If this ain't rock bottom,
Then, baby, bring me a shovel…
Or a snorkel
Because outside of this metaphor
I'm neck deep in debts
I've promised to myself
And all I've got before me is
A shriveled little dick
In lukewarm bath water.

Ah, but that's Friday night for you.

"When there's nothing left to burn, you have to set yourself on fire."

Help me set yourself on fire.
Help me burn down everything.
I want to watch you burn.
I never understood addiction until I met you.

Emotional Black Hole

It's been a long time since I've been in love.
I feel the absence in my chest these days —
A pit that will swallow all you have to give.
But I've already eaten all the planets around me,
And don't know if black holes die in the chasm of space.

A Million Billion Galaxies

My grasp on reality grows weak in the fall.
Death feels imminent for one and for all,
And I feel infinitesimally small,
Which makes me, somehow, infinitely large.
I take a breath and remind myself
That death is merely a corollary of time,
Without which we'd all be bugs,
Trapped in bubbles of amber —
    Beautiful glass baubles
    As distant as Andromeda.
But there is beauty in distant galaxies:
Their colorful veils of nebulous accretions
    And stars so bright
    They burn with the might
    Of a thousand scorching suns.
We are each of us a galaxy —
    Of mites and zen and the art
    Of aerobic respiration;
    Of chromosomes and bacteriophages,
    Molecular machines and electrical waves.
And we owe it to them to continue
If we expect the universe
To do the same for us.

John Carney

June 21, 2018

I know what
I am.
I think.
    COGITO.
I am a singular expression of that universal energy that
    ignites all life.
I am as temporary as a moment
    a smile
    the sound of a wave carried through the air to die
    when it strikes the inside of your ear.
I am ignorant — so ignorant! —
    an infant
I don't understand time or space or love,
    but I try and therefore I live.
    Yes —
I am ignorant. But
I won't echo that great voice that cries out in the night:
    "All
    I know is that
    I know nothing!"
I know one thing:
I know what
I am…
I think.

October 26, 2018

They say, "You'd rather be right than happy," as though there were really any choice.

My happiness left with her, on the other side of the door when she slammed it shut behind her.

I always hated that door with its uncountable layers of grey paint coated one on top of another.

I tell myself I hate her now — although that's not entirely true.

So what choice do I have left other than being right? What else is there to strive for when your happiness has absconded?

 Loneliness

I keep the television on.
The noise is almost a friend.
Almost.

There is a clock on the wall.
I watch the pendulum swing.
It is a mirror.

It is so lonesome underground.
And cold.
Memory fails me.

Looks like Stormy Weather

After the storm, my father said:
"You must be strong, my son."
Nobody knows, I wish I were dead —
They can't see what the storm has done.

A poster, a scarf, and the life that we'd made,
A smile, a wink, and her passing face —
I watched the deluge wash them away
And closed my heart to all merciful grace.

John Carney

Melancholy and Depression

Melancholy can be sweet —
>A twang of resentment
>A twinge of regret
And the song begins to rewrite itself
As a waltz that sinks and swells like a wave.

Depression is an altogether different monster.
Depression is a dirge that will carry you out the door with
>six sets of hands.
It is disease and addiction woven into wool and draped
>like a toga over imperial shoulders —
>>A gyre of a garment
>>A gargantuan *you-can't-win* beast.

The Bordello of Dolorous Fruits

I have these recurring drug-addled visions that I call
    the Bordello of Dolorous Fruits.

Strawberries, raspberries, blueberries too
And others of dubious smell or of hue.
They live in my mind,
    An absurd little tribe
Of sad and deranged little clowns.
Their features are strange,
Some are blind, some are lame,
But all of them dance to my tune.

And to what tragic ends do I rush off all these men
And women and children as well?
    To the edge of the earth,
    To the time before birth,
And down to the fires of Hell,
    Through the vacuum of space,
    Through the holes in white lace,
And along all the threads of the Fates.

John Carney

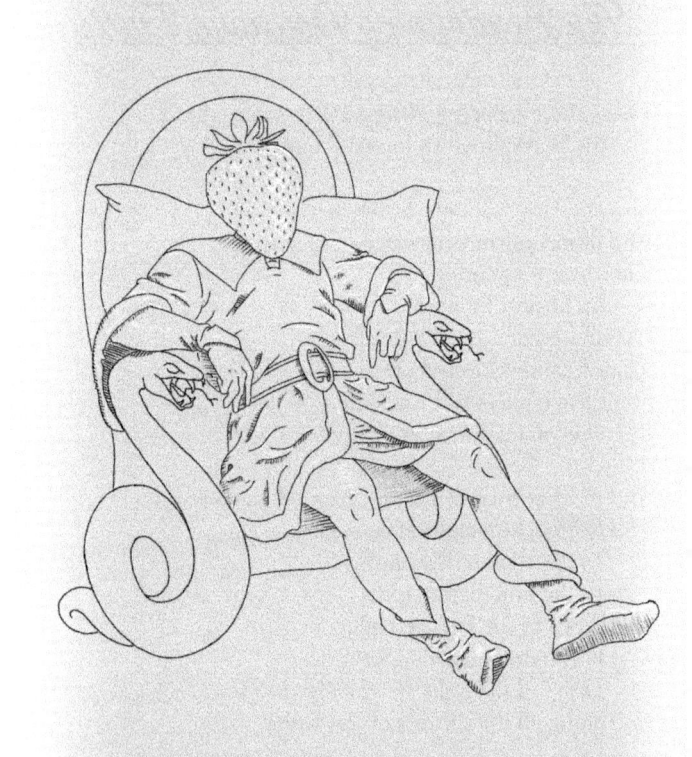

The Strawberry King (i)

The people have gathered, girding the street;
They're crowding to see the King's gilded feet.
Plain feet with ten toes, just like all the rest,
But since they're the King's, they must be the best.
These feet must be shielded and sheathed in gold.
The cost of his shoes could scarcely be told.
In a bowl in his hand, there the real sight,
A quivering pile, his dearest delight.

    Strawberries! Strawberries! Ripe and so red –
    Everyone stared at the juice that they bled.
    Strawberries! Strawberries! Not often seen,
    Yet e'er at hand since the death of his queen.

What of this queen who will soon be forgot,
Cast aside like a plucked 'forget-me-not'?
Ere it was she who was one of the serfs,
Who eat their plain meals upon their plain hearths.
Does no one recall how they adored her?
So kind and caring, young Queen Moxmori.
But sorrowful days of mourning have passed,
And the King is coming to break his fast.

    Women! Such women! From far and from wide,
    All congregated to be his next bride.
    Women! Such women! See nothing amiss,
    They've all set their sights on marital bliss,
For what could go wrong on a day such as this?

The Strawberry King (ii)

The women have come; they stand in a row.
They've been arrayed since before the cock's crow.
They wait in suspense, each sighing aloud,
Until a great cheer erupts from the crowd.
"The King!" "He's here!" His head bobs up and down.
Everyone stares at his Boeotian crown.
The King with his bowl, he sits and he grins.
The girls file past, and he pictures their sins.
 Strawberries! Strawberries! Scarlet and sweet,
 But sticky and soft, like pieces of meat.
 Strawberries! Strawberries! Stain his hands red,
 And increase his girth with each one he's fed.
He sees one he likes and stops the review.
Waves to come nearer, "My dear, who are you?"
She sits on his left. He pours her a drink.
She swallows it down with a deft little wink.
"My name is nobody," shrewdly she says.
Already he knows that she must be his.
The King will soon learn we reap what we've sown –
In the maid's hand sits a bowl of her own.
 Women! Such women! Beware of their scorn,
 Or else you will join the others they've shorn.
 Women! Such women! As the King's new madame,
 The girl who became Queen Elisiam –
Then disposed of the king like a paschal lamb.

<u>Pasiphaë and The Phalarian Bull</u>

I had a girl made my heart feel full,
Or just a dream that passed the days.
I should have called her Pasiphaë,
For I was just her bull.

I know another bull she deserves,
And nothing less to be tortured with:
The Brazen Bull of Sicilian myth!
I hope this for her Hell fore'er reserves.

Daedalus

Daedalus, Daedalus,
Wherefore art thou, Daedalus?
    And wherefore art thou works?
The Labyrinth, the Brazen Bull, and your child's corpse?
Which jeweled isle hides them now while you make your
    course?

The sea has swallowed up your son —
Some god's vengeance for what you've done.
    Now serve you another master,
    At least until the next disaster.

John Carney